CANCELLED

SMSF DIY guide

SMSF

DIY Guide

Everything you need to successfully set up and run your own self managed superannuation fund

Sam Henderson

Wrightbooks

First published in 2012 by Wrightbooks
an imprint of John Wiley & Sons Australia, Ltd
42 McDougall St, Milton Qld 4064
Office also in Melbourne

Typeset in Berkeley LT 11.3/14

© Sam Henderson 2012
The moral rights of the author have been asserted

National Library of Australia Cataloguing-in-Publication data:

Author:	Henderson, Sam.
Title:	SMSF DIY guide: everything you need to successfully set up and run your own self managed superannuation fund / Sam Henderson.
ISBN:	9780730377238 (pbk.)
Notes:	Includes index
Subjects:	Pension trusts—Australia—Management
	Retirement income—Australia
	Finance, personal—Australia
Dewey Number:	332.672540994

Cover design by Peter Reardon, Pipeline Design <www.pipelinedesign.com.au>

Cover image: istockphoto.com/©Alex Slobodkin

All Henderson Maxwell diagrams designed by Xander Creative for Henderson Maxwell.

Extracts from the 'Superannuation Industry (Supervision) Act 1993', Australian Government, ComLaw, 30 November 1993

Extracts from 'Self Managed Superannuation Funds Ruling', Australian Taxation Office, 21 April 2010

Tables on pages 13 and 140 © Australian Taxation Office (ATO). The aforementioned and all ATO information included in this publication was current at the time of publishing. Readers should refer to the ATO website <www.ato.gov.au> for up-to-date ATO information.

BT Material © BT Financial Group 2011. BTFG makes no representation as to the accuracy of the facts or assumptions made in the Copyright Work, or to the currency of the information and no company in the BT Financial Group or Westpac Banking Corporation Group (BT Group) accepts responsibility for the accuracy or completeness of the Copyright Work. The BT Group and its officers, directors, employees, representatives and agents are not liable for and are released from any loss or claim suffered or incurred by the Licensee, Publisher or a third party in connection with the inclusion of the Copyright Work in the Licensee Work. The Copyright Work is provided by way of information only and is not, and must not be relied upon as, financial, tax, legal or other advice. Neither BTFG nor any of its related bodies corporate have any obligation to provide any updated information to the Licensee or Publisher regarding the Copyright Work.

Printed in China by Printplus Limited

10 9 8 7 6 5 4 3 2 1

Disclaimer

Contents

Preface

Superannuation is such a huge opportunity for people to build their assets and reduce their tax, but it's poorly understood in Australia. I hope this book will make more people aware of its supreme benefits, which can make their lives so much better through improved decision making so they can achieve a state of financial wellbeing. I truly believe that if everyone had a better grasp of the superannuation system they would embrace its many advantages and retire earlier, with more money in their pocket.

I would be the first to gladly admit that money isn't everything in life, but it sure does help. It gives you more options and choices to do what you want. It may give you the ability to help others, contribute more to your community, and give your kids and grandkids more opportunity in years to come. Having money allows you to travel and have more experiences with other cultures and broaden your own horizons. If you have worked hard all your life, well-managed superannuation will give you the retirement you deserve.

I joke that 30 per cent of my client base is travelling around the country at any one time, but it's true. The grey nomads are keeping this country going, as caravan parks around this wide nation remain full to the brim. These people have worked hard and deserve a break, and superannuation is giving them a tax-free holiday—except for the cost of diesel!

This self managed superannuation fund (SMSF) book is an extension of my first book, *Financial Planning DIY Guide*. It aims at giving readers the opportunity to find methods and systems to build their assets faster by reducing tax, and increasing flexibility and control of their retirement savings. While SMSF is the fastest growing sector of superannuation—faster than industry and retail funds—the education gap remains significant, like the retirement savings gap.

SMSFs are where the money is, so it makes a sustainable business model for me personally, but, more importantly than that, through this book I want to help people engage with their superannuation and make better decisions about their money.

About the author

Sam Henderson is CEO and senior financial adviser at Henderson Maxwell, a fee-for-service, independently owned, boutique financial planning firm with offices in Sydney and Melbourne, that specialises in self managed super funds.

Sam has a commerce degree (specialising in accounting and financial planning), a diploma and advanced diploma of financial services and an advanced diploma of marketing management; he is currently working towards a master of commerce degree. He is also an accredited mortgage consultant, direct share specialist and an expert in self managed superannuation funds.

Sam is the author of the top-selling book *Financial Planning DIY Guide*, also published by Wiley.

He is the regular money-man on Channel 10's Logie-award winning program *The Circle* and is a regular host of Sky Business Channel's *Your*

Money, Your Call. He also regularly guest hosts Sky Business Channel's *First Business* and *Lunch Money*.

Sam regularly contributes to *Money* magazine, *The Australian Financial Review*, <www.afr.com>, the *Australian Women's Weekly*, *The Sydney Morning Herald*, *The Age*, *Financial Standard* and *Independent Financial Adviser* and *Asset* magazines. He is a frequent keynote speaker at the ASX Investor Success series, ASX DIY Super strategy days, Retirement Expo, and the Investment and Property Expos in both Sydney and Melbourne.

Sam is also a regular presenter and an expert in practice management within the financial planning industry, having spoken at the national Financial Planning Association Conference, Financial Standard Managed Accounts Conference, Dealers Group Conference, CPA Congress, Financial Wisdom Premium Practice Conference and many other industry conferences since 2004.

Sam has won a number of coveted industry awards, both individually and on a company level. He won a Financial Planning Association (FPA) Best Practice 2011 Award, and Securitor's New Financial Adviser of the year back in 2004. In 2009 Henderson Maxwell won *Asset* magazine's innovation award in the growth category after being highly recognised in 2007.

Sam is a family man with interests in surfing, snow skiing, boating and swimming.

For more on Sam Henderson see <www.samhenderson.com.au>, <www.thediyinvestor.com.au> or <www.hendersonmaxwell.com.au>. You can also follow him on Twitter @henderson_sam.

Acknowledgements

My key acknowledgements go to my immediate family. My beautiful wife, Jacqui, is always supportive of everything I do—except maybe surfing when I should be helping her out, but I need my outlets. Nevertheless, she is steadfast and strong, and maintains her own vision and direction in life. Together we make an incredible team and she remains my rock.

My little boy Louis (Loo-ee) is cute as a button and just six months old as I write this so we are still getting to know each other, but he's a special little fella. Aanika, who is four, is full of life and love. Unlike my last book, writing this one hasn't taken me away from the kids at all, as I have managed to spend a few days a week with the family. We have a lot of love in the Henderson household and that keeps us well bound together, albeit somewhat sleep deprived as we work Louis into a routine.

My fantastic staff remain loyal and hardworking and remarkably dedicated to the vision of independent financial advice to the true benefit of our clients. They continue to up-skill themselves and pursue their personal ambitions under my umbrella. Diana Chan has just achieved a top 20 spot in the *Asset* magazine Paraplanner of the Year Awards, which is a great achievement. No doubt she will improve her position as the competition continues. Diana's husband, Andrew Chan, has also been fantastic in his roles as business development and client manager and as a senior financial adviser.

Andrew Zbik has built on his education to take the next step into the media with his 2UE business report every Monday and Friday night, as well as a few stints on Sky Business Channel's *Your Money, Your Call*, *First Business* and *Lunch Money*. He is definitely the future of independent financial advice.

Pam Barnes (executive producer) and Kate Henry (segment producer) at Channel 10's Logie–award winning *The Circle* have been supportive of my ideas and angles on the many stories I have done for them over the past year or so.

The team at Sky Business have also been very supportive over the past few years, particularly Kylie Merritt, who has built Sky Business into the success it is today. My stints on *Your Money Your Call*, *First Business* and *Lunch Money* have helped build my profile.

Stuart Bocking at 2UE has been a huge supporter of Henderson Maxwell and my team, having us on his show every Monday and Friday night. There have been a few shows when I've had to lock myself in my car inside the garage so the kids can't be heard in the background.

Sally Patten at the *Australian Financial Review* and <www.afr.com> has been supportive of my many articles and regular position as a columnist on their website. She has also been patient when articles are late and poorly edited in my busier weeks. Thanks for your patience, Sally.

Lastly the team at Wiley has been incredibly patient and accommodating as I have pushed the boundaries on deadlines because of work and family commitments over the months of writing this book. So thanks, guys!

Superannuation basics

In an uncertain world, this can only strengthen Australia and make the outlook for its citizens much more secure.

Paul Keating, former prime minister and former treasurer of Australia, and the chief architect of superannuation in Australia

Let's face it, superannuation laws are complex and unless you like reading super legislation, like I do, you are probably busy just living your life, working and trying to take some time out. However, you don't have to be a tax or superannuation expert to understand super: this book is designed to guide you through the convoluted system of superannuation in the easiest way possible, based on the lifetime of experience and advice I have shared with my clients.

Superannuation is one of the most poorly understood investment structures in Australia, but it provides one of the best opportunities for investing in a tax-effective environment. Many people put super in the too hard basket and ignore it until just before retirement — when it is too late to resurrect — and miss out on the benefits super offers. Admittedly, superannuation is difficult to understand, with its constantly changing rules, but just a little research can make a big difference to the type of retirement you will have.

Many people tell me they don't trust superannuation, or that they think superannuation is just a scam to take 9 per cent of their hard-earned salary dollars. Some of these people are judging the superannuation system on the basis of how much their super earns—especially since the global financial crisis (GFC) of 2008. But their opinion often relates to how they have chosen to invest their super.

If your super had been invested in cash over the past few years, you would have gained at least a 50 per cent tax benefit if you had been salary sacrificing into super, and your balance would have risen by 7 per cent a year. Anyone investing in shares through their super in that time would have experienced a loss of up to 30 per cent, assuming they had around 50 to 70 per cent of their balance invested in shares, which is fairly common. Given that most people have a choice of super fund and a choice of how their money is invested in the fund, anyone suspicious of superannuation should make different investment choices and make sure that their choices match their risk profile. If they feel insecure, they should ensure their investments include more cash and fixed interest and less property and shares. In a self managed super fund you have complete control over how your money is invested. Whatever you do, don't confuse the benefits of investing through super with the performance of your investments.

As you will see in this chapter, superannuation presents fantastic opportunities to invest your hard-earned dollars while reducing or eliminating tax, while giving you the retirement you have dreamed of. Small changes in the way you distribute your income or invest your funds can make substantial differences at retirement.

What superannuation is—and is not

Superannuation is a savings vehicle that offers low tax rates and is specifically designed to help you save for your retirement. When the government designed the superannuation system in the early 1990s, it chose this low-tax investment structure to encourage people to save for their retirement so it wouldn't have to support everyone with the Age Pension.

Superannuation isn't a product that you can buy from an insurance company or fund manager (although it sometimes used to be, and you may even own one of these products offered before the government created the current super system). Super funds of all kinds operate as trusts, much like a family trust. A trust is an investment entity that is designed to hold and distribute assets and income to its beneficiaries.

Tax in super

Superannuation has its own tax rates. Tax on anything your super earns is just 15 per cent. Capital gains tax on an asset held inside a superannuation fund for more than 12 months is taxed at just 10 per cent. Once you reach age 60 and retire, or if you are drawing an income from your superannuation (that is, you are over age 55 and retired), no capital gains tax is charged on your assets in super. Once you reach age 60 and take your super, you pay no tax at all under the current legislation. Once you retire, no tax is charged against the super assets that provide your income. If you hold investments outside super, you will have to pay tax on anything they earn at what is called your marginal tax rate. That means you could pay 30 to 45 per cent income tax instead of 15 per cent tax in super (see table 1.1 and table 1.2, overleaf). For example, in 2011–12 earnings between $37 000 and $80 000 will be taxed at 30 per cent, between $80 000 and $180 000 will be taxed at 37 per cent, and any taxable income you earn over $180 000 will be taxed at 45 per cent. You can add another 1.5 per cent for the Medicare levy.

Table 1.1: marginal tax rates 2011–12

Taxable income	Tax on this income
0 – $6000	Nil
$6001 – $37 000	15c for each $1 over $6000
$37 001 – $80 000	$4650 plus 30c for each $1 over $37 000
$80 001 – $180 000	$17 550 plus 37c for each $1 over $80 000
$180 001 and over	$5 550 plus 45c for each $1 over $180 000

Source: <www.ato.gov.au>.

Table 1.2: taxation rates in superannuation

Description of type of super contribution	Superannuation tax
Concessional contributions—limited to $25 000 a year for under 50s and $50 000 a year for over 50s, e.g. through salary sacrifice	15%
Non-concessional contributions—limited to $150 000 a year or $450 000 averaged over three years, e.g. from an inheritance, windfall or asset sale	0%

If you contribute money to superannuation, you pay only 15 per cent contributions tax on your contribution if you make it before tax is deducted (a concessional contribution), compared with 30 per cent or even 45 per cent tax on your salary—that's a saving of 50 to 66 per cent. If you contribute after-tax money to super, say from a windfall, inheritance or with some spare cash, you pay no contributions tax at all (a non-concessional contribution), and you will pay no tax when you withdraw those funds in retirement.

As you can see in figure 1.1 superannuation attracts just 15 per cent tax on earnings, and an account-based pension (AP) has a zero tax rate, making super a very attractive structure through which to invest.

Figure 1.1: tax rates on the different investment structures

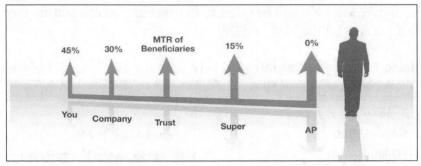

The laws that rule super

Superannuation is governed by several Commonwealth laws, including the *Superannuation Industry (Supervision) Act 1993* (SIS Act), *Income*

Tax Assessment Act 1997 (ITAA97), the *Corporations Act 2001, Tax Administration Act 1953* and the usual variety of case-law decisions from the outcome of specific cases, which set precedents for future court cases. To confuse things further, in May every year in the federal budget, the government announces some new changes to superannuation law, some of which make it through parliament and become law, and some of which never become law for a variety of reasons.

Superannuation is a very flexible structure that allows you to invest in a host of assets, including cash, fixed interest, Australian shares, international shares, options and warrants, or even physical assets, such as gold, commercial property or residential property.

Some of these assets also offer attractive tax concessions. For instance, shares in companies such as those listed on the Australian Securities Exchange (ASX) may pay dividends, providing an income for the investor. If the company has already paid 30 per cent company tax on those dividends, it attaches franking credits to the dividends, which represent the amount of tax the company has already paid on your behalf relative to the number of shares you own. You can then deduct that tax from your income tax if your shares are held outside super so you don't pay double the tax on that income—once by the company and then by you as the owner of the shares. However, if the shares are held in your super fund, and your tax rate is 15 per cent—or even 0 per cent if you are drawing an income stream—then you can actually get a tax refund from the ATO when you submit the tax return for your fund, because the company paid tax on your behalf at 30 per cent, but your lower tax rate in super means you are eligible to claim that tax back. This works for both fully managed superannuation funds and a self managed superannuation fund.

What superannuation is not

By definition, superannuation is not a managed fund. It is not a specific investment—just a tax-effective structure under which you invest.

Why you need superannuation

The Australian population over the age of 80 is set to quadruple by 2030, which will put significant stress on the country's welfare and health systems and aged care facilities. The simple fact is that you will to need to fund your own retirement if you want to enjoy the living standards you deserve or have enjoyed during your working life. With our ageing population and low-immigration policy, our government may not be able to support everyone on the Age Pension, which is why it offers tax incentives for you to self-fund your retirement. This is what superannuation is all about. If you want any quality of lifestyle after you retire, then some form of self-funding will be essential.

The Age Pension in 2011 paid singles just under $20000 a year and a little over $29000 for a couple. Compare those with the figures published by the ASFA Westpac Retirement Survey in its a report on living costs of retirees. In 2011 it said that, for a comfortable life in retirement, the average single needs just over $40000 a year and the average couple needs nearly $55000 a year (the study assumes they own their home). The difference between the Age Pension and what the average couple needs is what I call the retirement savings gap. In Australia, the retirement savings gap is massive.

Let me paint the picture of the average Australian couple at retirement. They are aged 65 and can't afford to retire earlier. The average couple retires with around $230000 in superannuation: men average a super payout of about $150000 and women average half that, at about $75000. Women have a lower level of savings for several reasons, including time out of the paid workforce to raise children and the fact that women make up a large proportion of part-time workers. The super guarantee started in only 1993 and it was a mere 3 per cent of salary before it grew to 9 per cent by 2002, so many older Australians, male and female, haven't seen the full benefits of superannuation. If the aforementioned couple draws around 6 per cent each year of their superannuation at retirement, they would be withdrawing $13800 per year, and receive the full Age Pension. Their super falls below the lower threshold for the Age Pension's assets test (indexed up every March and September) of around $265000. When their super income is combined with their Centrelink benefit, they can expect to live on around $35000 to $40000 year, unless they choose to continue to work, which many do.

Many of these people will be used to living on a household income of $60000 to $80000 a year, or more, before retirement, and they will struggle to manage their household budgets in retirement, let alone be able to afford private health insurance, home health care or elective surgery for things like hip or knee replacements, to name a just few issues they might encounter in the future.

Compared with the average retiree, self managed superannuation members average $450000 each in their super fund and have a combined fund of around $900000. Although this group makes up only 3 per cent of the population, they account for more than 35 per cent of the $1.4 trillion in superannuation in Australia. On average, they will be able to enjoy a comfortable retirement, being able to draw a retirement income of more than $52000 a year from their super, and they typically own their own home. Interestingly, with the regular upwards indexing of the Age Pension assets test, the average SMSF member/trustee would be eligible for the Age Pension if their combined assets, excluding their residence, were under $1 million (the upper limit for the assets test in September 2011 was $1018000 for a home-owning couple and $686000 for singles, and these thresholds will continue to rise every six months).

Self managed superannuants are drawn from across the Australian population, ranging from small business owners to executives, professionals and academics. There is no typical self managed superannuant profile, but members of self managed super funds generally have higher levels of education and earn more than the average Australian income of about $65000 a year.

Self managed super fund members share other qualities, too, such as wanting better control of their superannuation and to be party to the decision making that affects their future.

If you want a comfortable retirement, you will need to be at least partially self funded, and I think a self managed super fund is the ideal vehicle to achieve this outcome. To run a self managed super fund you will need a clearly defined plan for it, and you will also need to assemble a trusted team to help you with the administration and investment decisions of your fund, including an accountant, an auditor and possibly a financial adviser. You will also need a basic understanding of the superannuation system and its rules and regulations.

This book is all about helping you to navigate the superannuation system and to provide a guide to help you make better decisions about your financial future so you can spend more time doing what you enjoy. I will not be advocating running your self managed super fund as a second job as I want you to enjoy your life and have a great retirement. Self managed super is not about managing your funds every day, or trading shares or speculating in property. It's about setting goals, establishing a strategy and carefully, but not obsessively, managing your funds in a way that matches your attitude towards risk. A self managed super fund is essentially a tax-minimisation strategy combined with a risk management project to fund your retirement.

Yes, superannuation can be confusing

Superannuation laws change regularly and it's hard to keep up with those changes unless you work in the industry or have a penchant for reading superannuation law. Most people don't follow these regular changes or understand how those changes affect them. The result is that people are disengaged from their own retirement savings—possibly their biggest asset outside their own home.

Although superannuation is complex, it is becoming a more attractive investment structure because of the tax concessions it affords. Many investments decisions should be considered under the structure of superannuation because of these tax concessions. For example, you can now borrow money inside a self managed super fund and buy property, and when you sell the property, there is a likelihood that no capital gains tax will be payable.

If you do not have the time or inclination to manage your superannuation, then I strongly suggest that you seek advice from an independent financial adviser who will be well placed to give you unadulterated advice. Your accountant or self managed super fund administrators may also be able to assist you. Take ownership of your superannuation and seek advice when you have questions.

> **Never a silly question**
>
> There is no such thing as a silly question when it comes to your own money. Too many people don't ask questions because they worry about seeming ignorant. Because most people have a poor understanding of superannuation and taxation, they never feel comfortable about seeking information or asking questions. But it's your money, so you should never feel silly asking questions about it!

Superannuation is your opportunity to supercharge your investments. It offers a fantastic opportunity to increase your assets faster because one of the greatest inhibitors to investment growth—tax—is significantly lessened or eliminated. Your assets will grow more quickly because the income they produce is concessionally taxed. Lower tax rates do not increase the capital growth of an asset—that's up to the forces of the market in which you are invested—but when it comes to selling the asset any capital gains tax is lessened or nullified. At the end of the day, that means more money in your super.

Contributions—getting money into superannuation

Money gets into the super system in a number of ways and through a few payment methods. You can make contributions yourself and, if you are working, your employer has to contribute on your behalf as well. This section will describe the methods of making contributions and the benefits of contributing to super.

Superannuation guarantee

If you earn more than $450 per month your employer must put an additional amount of 9 per cent of your salary into a complying superannuation fund within 28 days of the end of each quarter until you reach age 70 (from 1 July 2013 the age limit will be removed). This is the law and employers who do not abide by these regulations are penalised. Your employer receives a tax deduction for your superannuation contributions.

If you are aged less than 50, your employer only has to put up to $25 000 into your fund — if you earn more than $277 778 per annum (lucky you!) then your super contributions will be capped at $25 000. It is currently proposed that the cap for people aged over 50 should be $50 000 a year until 2012, and that cap will continue after 2012 for people who have less than $500 000 in their super account.

Making contributions yourself

There are number of ways of getting money into superannuation, but before you make a contribution, you need to know that there are two types of contributions you can make: concessional and non-concessional.

Concessional contributions

Concessional contributions are made from your income before you pay tax on it. They include salary sacrifice contributions by employees (made from their before-tax salary) and tax-deductible contributions by self-employed people who earn 10 per cent or more of their earnings from self-employed activities (this is known as the 10 per cent rule). Self-employed people can make these contributions as lump sums, but generally employees can only make their contributions as they earn their income, and can only make lump-sum concessional contributions if they earn a bonus.

If you make a concessional contribution, you will pay 15 per cent tax on the money when it goes into the fund (contributions tax), instead of paying tax at your marginal tax rate, which can be up to 45 per cent. If your highest marginal tax rate is greater than 15 per cent then it would be beneficial to put money into superannuation if you have excess cash flow. This is the basis of the term salary sacrifice, because you can save your money in super and pay less tax, but you will have less cash from your pay and you cannot touch your super until you meet a condition of release.

Self-employed people can make their superannuation contributions at the end of the year to manage their tax better.

Concessional contributions used to be known as deductible contributions. They are also sometimes called before-tax contributions.

How to reduce your capital gains tax

If you are over the age of 55 and under the age of 65, and retired, you are considered to be self-employed as 10 per cent or more of your income will come from self-employment activities (simply because you will receive no income from employment sources). If you sell a property or shares to move money into superannuation, you can reduce your capital gains tax by making a contribution to superannuation of up to $50 000.

If you are employed, you can reduce the amount of capital gains tax payable on the sale of an asset by making salary sacrifice contributions throughout the year to maximise your concessional contributions and pay just 15 per cent tax on your income instead of 30 per cent, 37 per cent or 45 per cent tax: a saving of up to 67 per cent!

Non-concessional contributions

Non-concessional contributions are made from money you have already paid tax on (unless it was an inheritance, windfall or compensation payment that is not taxable). When a non-concessional contribution is paid into your super fund, you pay no contributions tax on it.

Non-concessional contributions were previously known as undeducted contributions. They are also sometimes called after-tax contributions.

There are also limits on the amount of non-concessional contributions you can make to your super. They are limited to $150 000 a year, though they can be averaged over three years (see table 1.3).

Table 1.3: superannuation contributions limits

Age	Concessional limit	Non-concessional limit
Under 50	$25 000	$150 000 a year or $450 000 (three-year average)
Over 50 but under 65	$50 000	$150 000 per annum or $450 000 (three-year average)
Over 65 but under 75*	$50 000	$150 000
Over 75	$0	$0

* Over-65s must meet the work test to make a contribution to super; that means they must work at least 40 hours in any 30 consecutive days in the financial year in which they want to make a contribution to super.

How to get money out of super

When you need access to your superannuation money to create an income stream at retirement or just to access a lump sum, it must be done legally, otherwise the ramifications can be far-reaching, including fines, an increased superannuation penalty tax of 46.5 per cent, or even a jail sentence. These penalties can be strictly applied owing to the tax concessions afforded to superannuation and the temptation it may create by superannuants to exploit its benefits.

Conditions of release

You can withdraw money from superannuation only if you can meet a condition of release. The Australian Taxation Office (ATO) regulates SMSFs in Australia and it is very much focused on this little piece of legislation. The ATO does not want people to access their superannuation before they are eligible to do so, and it has demonstrated a willingness and conviction to prosecute those who try to contravene the super rules.

For the same reason, you must take care not to mix your own money with your super fund's money. Your superannuation is a separate trust and it's assets need to be quarantined from your own as each entity, your superannuation and your personal assets, is treated differently for tax purposes. You will not only have to explain yourself to the ATO if they audit your fund, but you also need to have an independent auditor sign-off on the operations of your fund each year before your tax return is completed. Your auditor has an obligation to report any anomalies to the ATO—so you have been warned.

Conditions of release include:

¤ reaching your preservation age

¤ reaching age 65 (whether you are working or not)

¤ being aged 55 to 64 and retired (working fewer than 10 hours a week)

¤ taking a transition to retirement pension, whether you are still working or not (limited to a maximum of 10 per cent of your super balance for those aged over 55—see chapter 9 for more information about this)

◻ financial hardship (very strict rules and regulations)

◻ death

◻ disablement (permanent or temporary)

◻ your benefits being less than $200

◻ terminal medical condition

◻ compassionate grounds.

Preservation age

Your preservation age is the age at which you can retire and legally gain access to your superannuation money. Naturally, you can retire earlier—in fact, you can retire whenever you want—but you will not have access to your superannuation money, so you will need to live on funds held outside of the superannuation environment until you meet a formal condition of release.

Depending on what year you were born, your preservation age will vary. As you can see in table 1.4, for those born before 1 July 1960, preservation age is 55. For those born after 1 July 1960, preservation age increases.

Table 1.4: preservation ages

Date of birth	Preservation age
Before 1 July 1960	55
1 July 1960 – 30 June 1961	56
1 July 1961 – 30 June 1962	57
1 July 1962 – 30 June 1963	58
1 July 1963 – 30 June 1964	59
From 1 July 1964	60

Source: <www.ato.gov.au>.

Withdrawing lump sums

Once you meet a condition of release you can access your super as a lump sum, or as a pension (income stream) or a combination of the two. When you withdraw your benefits, you may have to pay tax on the amount you withdraw. The amount of tax you will have to pay depends on your age (you will pay no tax on super withdrawals once you reach age 60, for instance) and the categories into which your super money falls. These categories are shown on the superannuation statements you get from your fund each year.

Preserved benefits

Preserved benefits are benefits you are not allowed to access until you meet a condition of release. Once you have met a condition of release, you will be able to withdraw your money, which is likely to include components on which you will have to pay tax, and those on which no tax is payable (see below). Most of your super money is likely to be preserved.

Restricted non-preserved benefits

Restricted non-preserved benefits are fairly rare. They include money you or an employer contributed to super for you before 1999. This amount is frozen at the amount it was when the rules changed in that year. You may be able to access these benefits if you leave a current employer; otherwise you will need to meet a condition of release to access these funds.

Unrestricted non-preserved benefits

Unrestricted non-preserved benefits are also made up of superannuation money contributed before 1999, and this amount was also frozen at 1999 levels. You can access this part of your benefit without having to meet a condition of release — you can withdraw this money from your fund at any time. Once you have met a condition of release, then all your super benefits fall into the unrestricted non-preserved category, and you will have access to your super money at any time.

Taxable benefits

Taxable benefits are made up of contributions that were taxed at 15 per cent when they went into your fund, and they include your employer's 9 per cent superannuation guarantee, your salary sacrifice contributions and other concessional contributions made by the self-employed. These benefits used to be known as deductible super contributions.

If you meet a condition of release and are under age 60, the first $165 000 of these benefits are free of tax (the amount increases each year in line with increases in average weekly ordinary time earnings (AWOTE) that exceed $5000, so this amount rises in increments of $5000). Amounts over the tax-free threshold are taxed at 16.5 per cent (15 per cent plus the Medicare levy) up to age 60, then become tax-free. If a fund member dies and these benefits are passed on to independent adult children or beneficiaries, they are also taxed at 16.5 per cent, even if the member would have paid no tax if they had withdrawn these benefits. (It's a good idea to have a power of attorney in place, so that your attorney can cash out your super before death.)

Non-taxable benefits

Non-taxable benefits are made up of the non-concessional contributions you have paid into your super fund from after-tax money. This portion used to be called an undeductible component. You pay no tax on this money when it goes into the fund and it remains free of tax when it is withdrawn. The assumption is that you have paid tax on the money already. For example, if you sell an asset and contribute the money to super (assuming capital gains tax is paid by you personally) or if you have a windfall, such as a Lotto win, and contribute the lump sum to super (within the contribution limit laws), you will not have to pay 15 per cent contributions tax.

No tax is paid on lump sums once you reach age 60 or when a member is allowed to withdraw their super because they are terminally ill.

Income streams

Once you reach a condition of release and decide to retire, you may prefer to start an income stream from your superannuation. In this case you simply set up a direct debit payment facility from your super fund's bank account to your personal account or accounts. You need to ensure you have enough cash in your fund to pay pensions, so you may need to sell assets held in your super fund or buy assets with high income to pay your income stream over time (see chapters 9 and 10 for more information on income streams). How you will support the payment of pensions from your SMSF must be detailed in your investment strategy.

A number of different types of income streams are possible (see chapters 9 and 10 for more information and some examples of how each of them works). Examples of income streams include:

¤ account-based pensions (formerly known as allocated pensions)

¤ transition to retirement income streams (or pensions)

¤ term allocated pensions

¤ defined benefit pensions (more common for government employees who are members of state and Commonwealth super schemes).

Income streams are tax-free for people over the age of 60, except for some defined benefit pensions that remain taxable (usually because no tax has been paid on the super funds while they have been building up—which is known as the accumulation phase). For people under the age of 60 but over 55, who have met a condition of release and are eligible to draw an account-based pension or a transition to retirement pension, the income stream is added to their taxable income, but they receive a 15 per cent tax rebate on that income, which in many cases eliminates or lowers the tax significantly.

As a trustee of an SMSF, you should make sure that your trust deed allows for the different types of income streams that you may consider paying in the future. If your trustee deed is more than three years old, an update may be necessary, as superannuation laws can change rapidly. This may cost around $500, but it is worth the cost.

Key points

¤ Superannuation is a savings environment designed to fund your retirement that offers lower rates of taxation than other forms of saving.

¤ Super is not a product—rather it is a structure under which you invest in a host of different investment options.

¤ Super offers some incredible tax benefits. One example is that, once you have retired, you will pay no income tax on pensions, no earnings tax on interest, dividends or rent, and no capital gains tax on the assets sold within the SMSF.

¤   Make sure you understand how to make contributions to superannuation to maximise your tax benefits and reduce your chance of penalties for non-compliance in your SMSF.

¤   Concessional contributions include salary sacrifice and super guarantee payments. They are limited to $25 000 a year for under-50s, and $50 000 a year for over-50s who have less than $500 000 in their member balance.

¤   Non-concessional contributions are not taxed on the way in or out of your fund and are limited to $150 000 per person a year. This amount can also be averaged over three years so that a lump sum of $450 000 can be contributed in one year, with no more non-concessional contributions permitted for the subsequent two years. This is known as the three-year averaging provision.

¤   Check your annual super statements and understand what the following terms mean: preserved, restricted non-preserved, non-restricted non-preserved, taxable and non-taxable.

¤   Super income streams and lump sums are tax-free for over-60s, but usually attract low levels of tax for under-60s who have met a condition of release.

¤   Make sure your trust deed is up to date and allows for different types of income streams or future changes to superannuation law.

CHAPTER 2

Is a self managed super fund right for you?

Self managed super funds (SMSFs) are now the largest and fastest-growing segment of the super industry.
Michael D'Ascenzo, Commissioner of Taxation

A self managed super fund isn't for everyone, but if you're looking for greater control, transparency, accountability and flexibility for your super money then it may be the right choice for you.

Many prospective SMSF members are fed up with the low cash returns from their existing super fund, sharemarket volatility and the fact that they have no idea of where their industry or retail super funds are being invested, and no control over their fund's investment decisions. One large state super fund owned the Cross City Tunnel in Sydney, which went broke. A previously top-performing industry fund lost $1.6 billion of its funds in 2009 in the financial crisis through poor investment choice. Gyrating sharemarkets, where most of your superannuation has traditionally been invested, have exacerbated this problem for industry, retail and corporate super funds, and fuelled a lack of faith in management and transparency of investment decisions.

Many clients of financial advisers have also sought alternative and cheaper super management structures, such as SMSFs, so they can take control of their own funds with the aim of reducing the fees they pay and increasing their returns.

While investment returns have been fluctuating wildly, particularly over the last few years, the one thing you can control is costs. It is a financial reality that, if you reduce costs, you can increase your returns, so there has been a flood of new SMSFs set up by people exiting traditional financial planning products, such as managed funds, that sit on expensive and unnecessary wrap platforms (software that allows the trading, management and reporting of managed funds) managed by financial advisers.

Naturally I have a concern that people who set up SMSFs will struggle to manage their investments effectively over the long term, but many have been so fearful of sharemarkets that they have simply transferred their super from their existing fund into their new SMSF as cash. These funds remain in cash to this day. While I don't think this is good money management, it may allow the SMSF members to sleep better at night, resting assured that their hard-earned dollars are not at the mercy of an organisation that they feel may not have their best interests in mind.

My job is to help SMSF members manage their investments better and meet their underlying goals and objectives. A key objective of financial planning is cash flow management and tax reduction, and an SMSF provides the perfect structure through which to invest, no matter how share or property markets perform, because in an SMSF, the investment strategy is entirely up to the SMSF's members and it can be tailored to meet member objectives. In any case, there may be better performing fixed interest options than holding your money in cash for sharemarket-shy investors.

What is a self managed super fund?

As you learnt in chapter 1, superannuation is a savings environment designed specifically to fund your retirement and to look after your beneficiaries, while offering the incentive to save via concessional tax rates.

A self managed superannuation fund (also known as a DIY super fund) is a private investment trust established specifically to fund retirement for you and the other members of the fund. An SMSF may have up to four members, who are also trustees of the fund, managing their own retirement savings.

Trustees of SMSFs have to meet a number of regulatory obligations, including providing annual tax returns, maintaining accurate accounts, managing pensions, getting the fund audited each year and managing the fund's investments. A fund may cost between $1000 and $5000, or even more, in annual compliance costs, in addition to any advice and investment costs that have to be paid.

The members must construct an investment strategy for the fund and manage its assets (see chapter 4 for a detailed example of an investment strategy).

SMSFs have the most involved and engaged members in superannuation, and the single largest share of funds. While only 3 per cent of people (in 400 000 funds) are members of an SMSF, the sector makes up 37 per cent of all funds held in superannuation. The average fund balance is currently around $900 000, with an average member balance of $450 000.

SMSFs are regulated by the Australian Taxation Office (ATO), whereas other super funds are regulated by the Australian Prudential Regulation Authority (APRA). The trustees of an SMSF have to report annually to the ATO. The ATO has a specific list of around 90 rules and obligations that SMSFs have to abide by (see chapter 4), but the defining piece of legislation requires that the purpose of an SMSF is principally for retirement saving purposes—this is known as the sole purpose of an SMSF. You may not operate a business inside a self managed fund or have access to the funds to receive a personal benefit before you meet a condition of release (see chapter 1).

Why is the number of SMSFs growing so rapidly?

Self managed super funds are extremely popular and the number of SMSFs is growing faster than any other sector of superannuation. One reason for this is that SMSFs provide members with a greater sense of control and flexibility to manage their retirement savings.

There are about 450 000 SMSFs in Australia and around 25 000 to 30 000 new funds are set up each year (see table 2.1).

It has been interesting to watch the number of SMSFs established rise considerably in the face of sharemarket volatility and changes to the superannuation legislation providing tax minimisation opportunities for superannuants. It clearly illustrates that investors are wanting more than the retail and industry super funds can provide. Interestingly, the 'more' that people seek is actually simplicity, because if you go to the ATO website at <www.ato.gov.au> and look at the asset allocation of SMSFs, you can see SMSF funds are predominantly invested in Australian shares and cash. A smaller proportion is invested in direct property than you may think. It may be said that investors want more clarity, transparency and control of their destiny, but more than ever they want certainty, and that is demonstrated by the high allocation of SMSF funds to cash and term deposits in a time when sharemarket investment has been less than favourable.

Tip

If you want to know more about self managed super funds, visit the ATO website and click on the link to Self Managed Super Funds Home at <www.ato.gov.au/superfunds>.

How an SMSF can save you money

When you are assessing the cost of running an SMSF, it's important that you differentiate between cost and value. Around 50 per cent of SMSF trustees seek advice from a financial adviser or investment adviser, but that is the area in which costs can be saved. Any cost saving is an increase in your return, hence the relationship to value. If you don't feel confident investing for yourself, then seek advice.

Table 2.1: trends in establishments of SMSFs 2004–2011

SMSF	June 2004	June 2005	June 2006	June 2007	June 2008	June 2009	June 2010	June 2011
Establishments	28142	21791	23658	44854	32189	31567	29609	33106
Wind-ups	4856	5081	5009	4089	5270	7987	5796	487
Net establishments	23286	16710	18649	40765	26919	23580	23813	32619
Total number of SMSFs	273417	290127	308776	349541	376460	400040	423853	456472
Total members SMSFs	525845	557646	592530	668234	713471	760674	805978	867863

Source: <www.ato.gov.au>.

23

Alternatively, here are three costs that SMSFs could avoid:

¤   management fees charged by financial advisers, which can be up to 1 per cent of funds under management every year

¤   wrap fees—a wrap is a software program used by an adviser providing tax reports and allowing trading of managed funds on your behalf, which can equate to 0.1 per cent to 0.88 per cent of funds under management each year

¤   managed funds fees—known as management expense ratios (MERs) or investment cost ratios (ICRs) that range from 0.3 per cent to 1.54 per cent, or even more.

Advantages and disadvantages of an SMSF

SMSFs have some advantages over other superannuations funds, but they might not suit everyone.

Advantages

The principal advantages of SMSFs are:

¤   better control over your retirement savings

¤   reduction in investment fees

¤   more choice in investment products, such as shares and residential property

¤   being able to invest directly in assets such as shares and property, and other physical assets such as gold

¤   the ability to borrow money to buy shares and property

¤   the ability to transfer shares (soon to be outlawed) and commercial property you own outside super into the fund

¤   flexibility to do what you want (within the superannuation laws)

¤   more flexibility in the way you invest

¤   better returns historically than retail and industry funds because of overweights to Australian shares and cash inside SMSFs (this can change over time).

Disadvantages

The principal disadvantages of SMSFs are:

⊠ cost of fees to meet the compliance requirements of an SMSF, such as administration, annual statements for members and an annual audit

⊠ having to find and pay for assistance to run the fund

⊠ responsibility for managing the funds

⊠ legal responsibility for managing the retirement savings of other fund members

⊠ difficulty of running the fund if you have little or no understanding of investment markets

⊠ having to pay penalties if the fund does not comply with the rules.

How much money do you need to set up an SMSF?

While the ATO suggests that the minimum balance needed to set up an SMSF is around $200 000, there is no legislated amount and it is possible to set up one for less, but your management fees may be higher as a percentage of the assets inside the fund. The $200 000 threshold suggested by the ATO includes the combined funds of all members. For instance, you should allow about $2000 to $4000 a year for the cost of accounting and the annual audit by a professional or specialist organisation. Your intention should be to try to keep the fees to less than 2 per cent per year.

I typically advise clients that if they have more than $100 000 in combined assets (husband and wife, or other members) and the ability to make substantial contributions up to the level of the contribution caps ($25 000 per year for under-50s and $50 000 per year for over 50s), then it may be worth setting up an SMSF with just $100 000 or even less. If they are not making contributions, then a recommended amount of around $300 000 or more would be more appropriate. The theory behind this suggestion is that if you are interested in having an SMSF and you will soon reach the ATO's suggested threshold of $200 000, then it is certainly plausible to set up one earlier than later.

Other types of superannuation funds

In addition to SMSFs, Australians have their super in a variety of funds, including retail funds, corporate funds, industry funds, defined-benefit funds and small APRA funds. Each type of fund has its advantages and disadvantages and your role is to find the one that best suits you and your financial goals.

Retail super fund

Retail super funds are available to everyone and may be supported by financial advisers and financial institutions. A retail super fund has an internal trustee. These funds are regulated by APRA. Retail super funds include old-style legacy retail superannuation funds (which paid trail commissions to advisers), and master trusts and wrap accounts that allow investors to access wholesale managed funds and direct shares without having to go into an SMSF. Retail funds do tend to be the more expensive option of those listed above, but they may come with advisers and plenty of investment choice. Examples of retail fund providers include BT (Westpac), Colonial First State (Commonwealth Bank), MLC (NAB), Asgard (Westpac) and Macquarie Wrap (Macquarie Bank).

The advantages of retail super funds include:

¤   choice of investments, including access to wholesale managed funds without trail commissions

¤   access to financial advisers who can help you to reduce tax and boost your super

¤   tax reporting completed for you

¤   online daily access to your accounts.

The disadvantages of retail super funds include:

¤ cost—they tend to be more expensive than other super funds

¤ no access to direct assets such as investment property

¤ most advisers use a set and forget strategy that doesn't give you active portfolio management

¤ underperformance caused by the level of fees.

Corporate super funds

Usually associated with your employer, corporate super funds have their own trustees and are regulated by APRA. They have developed more choice and lower fees over the years, and some also have a defined-benefit structure that offers employees a multiple of their final average salary at retirement in addition to any further contributions they have put into the fund. Defined benefit funds can be fantastic, and a huge boon for retirees, but very few employers run these today because of the expense; most employers have moved to an industry-style fund or a retail fund. Examples include services provided by companies such as Mercer, Russell, Plum and more directly via Telstra Super.

The advantages of corporate super funds:

¤ the defined-benefit component can be a huge advantage, far outweighing any or all of the disadvantages

¤ some choice of investments exist in certain funds.

The disadvantages of corporate super funds:

¤ cost

¤ poor service and limited advice owing to an institutional-style service provision

¤ generally a lack of choice of investments, such as limited direct share, cash or property options.

Industry super fund

Industry funds are not-for-profit superannuation funds associated with and run by a specific industry, although most are now open to everyone. Industry funds have an internal trustee and are regulated by APRA.

They tend to have low fees and limited advice services (although many now offer access to financial advisers) and appear to be appropriate to those members associated with a particular industry (before the introduction of super choice). They may also attract members who have lower account balances and who may be disengaged or disenfranchised from the superannuation industry and do not seek advice. Examples of industry funds include Australian Super, CBus for the building and construction industry, HESTA (Health Employees Superannuation Trust Australia) and REST (Retail Employees Superannuation Trust).

The advantages of industry funds include:

¤   simple superannuation solutions

¤   good service

¤   low fees

¤   cheap life, TPD and income protection insurance

¤   financial advice now offered by most funds

¤   generally improved investment choice in recent years

¤   all profits are returned to members—they are not-for-profit funds.

The disadvantages of industry super funds include:

¤   limited financial advice with limited tax advice

¤   limited choice of investments, although this is improving

¤   limited control for members, but similar to retail and corporate funds.

Defined benefit funds

These are usually state and federal government, or older company funds that offer a guaranteed lump sum or pension to their members at retirement. They are expensive for companies and the government, so these institutions have been trying to move members out of these products for years, and where these funds still exist it is rare for them to accept new members. If you are a member of a defined benefit fund, it offers huge benefits. I would rarely advise someone to exit a defined benefit fund unless they had a large debt that could be repaid by a lump sum or if they were gravely ill. An alternative for some owners of defined benefit pensions who need lump sums to repay debt is to cash out a portion to repay debt, and then continue to receive a smaller defined benefit income stream.

A member of a defined benefit fund may, for example, be entitled to an amount equal to 8.25 times their final average salary over the three years prior to retirement after a predetermined period of employment. Alternatively, they may be eligible to a set payment each fortnight, indexed to the Consumer Price Index (CPI), for the rest of their life and, if the member dies, a surviving dependant receives 66 per cent of the deceased's pension.

These funds have an internal trustee and are regulated by APRA. Examples include Commonwealth Superannuation Scheme, ESS and State Super Scheme (SSS).

The advantages of defined-benefit funds include:

¤ A guaranteed lump sum or income stream at retirement, so no retirement planning is required.

¤ No fluctuation in super balance as a result of sharemarket volatility.

¤ Indexed income streams are typically linked to inflation (UK pensions, paid to Australian citizens, are not indexed)!

¤ Lump sums are often augmented by member contributions for those who choose to salary sacrifice further.

The disadvantages of defined-benefit funds include the following:

¤ Generally, when a member dies, the income stream is lost, leaving nothing to the estate, which can be a problem. Only the spouse can receive a defined benefit income stream of around 66 per cent to the end of his or her life; other dependants, such as children, are not eligible to receive income streams from the deceased, and the benefits are lost forever.

¤ Lump sums obtain no benefit from a rising sharemarket.

¤ Some defined benefit pensions are not indexed.

¤ Often members cannot put additional contributions or investments into the fund.

Small APRA fund

While rarely used, a small APRA fund (SAF) is like a self managed fund, but it has an external trustee and is regulated by APRA. SAFs may be appropriate for SMSF members who are going overseas and cannot meet the regulatory requirements for residency. They may also suit someone who wants the investment choice possible through an SMSF without having to meet the compliance obligations themselves.

The advantages of small APRA funds include:

¤   suitability for people who have legal disabilities, such as compensation recipients

¤   flexibility for investment

¤   management of compliance paperwork for members by the trustee

¤   possibility for SMSF members to move into a fund if they move overseas

¤   simplicity of estate planning (spouses can receive tax-free reversionary pensions)

¤   suitability for members of an SMSF who have been disqualified, for example, when a member moves overseas for more than two years

¤   low compliance risks.

The disadvantages of small APRA funds include the following:

¤   members experience some loss of member control

¤   trustee needs to sign all cheques and documentation, which takes more time and effort

¤   trustee can place limitations of certain investments

¤   an external trustee will create an additional cost

¤   not widely used (only about 3500 in Australia).

Super choice: moving from one fund to another

It is simple to move your money from one super fund to another — this is called a superannuation rollover. A rollover is not considered a contribution to super as the funds are already inside the superannuation system, so no additional tax will have to be paid when the money is transferred. Most funds have a standard rollover form for you to complete to allow you to roll your money in or out of their fund. An SMSF member can use this standard form (plus a copy of their SMSF compliance certificate) to roll over their super balance into their SMSF.

Choice of fund in superannuation was introduced some years back and unless you have an employment contract that prohibits choice or you are a member of a defined benefit scheme that is exempt from the super choice legislation, then you will be eligible to choose your own fund.

Your employer must give you a superannuation choice form to allow you to choose your super fund, giving you more freedom as to where your work superannuation is directed. The ATO website has more choice of fund forms: type the words 'superannuation choice form' into the search engine at <www.ato.gov.au> to find the form.

Tips for running a better SMSF

There are plenty of pitfalls that need to be avoided in running an SMSF, which is why I always recommend that you use professionals to assist you to manage your fund. It is also the reason that I say SMSFs are not for everyone. A professional accountant or specialist SMSF administrator will be able to guide you through the compliance regime to ensure that, if you do raise eyebrows at the ATO and receive an audit, you will survive unscathed.

While chapter 3 will help build your education on the compliance requirements for the successful management of your SMSF, here are some top tips to help you run a better SMSF.

- Make sure you seek the assistance of an accountant or a specialist administrator to help you run a compliant fund. (See my website at <www.samhenderson.com.au> for more information on getting better advice for your SMSF.)

(cont'd)

Tips for running a better SMSF *(cont'd)*

- Do not take money out of your fund until you have confirmed with your accountant or administrator that you are allowed to do so. One of the key objectives of the ATO is to ensure people do not attempt to access their superannuation without meeting a legitimate condition of release (see chapter 1). You will be heavily penalised via fines, additional tax or even jail, if you are caught breaking the rules.

- As soon as your trust deed has been prepared, and before you start investing, ensure you have a written investment strategy that dictates the method and manner of investing your SMSFs funds. Over time, make sure you update it (see chapter 4 for details).

- Before you set up an SMSF make sure you understand the compliance requirements and ensure you are committed to the process by comparing the other types of super funds that may be available to you, and what their costs will be. SMSFs are not for everyone.

Key points

- ¤ SMSFs provide greater control, flexibility, transparency and accountability for members.

- ¤ An SMSF is a tax-effective private investment trust with up to four members, specifically designed to fund their retirement.

- ¤ There are more than 450 000 SMSFs in Australia and numbers are growing rapidly.

- ¤ Retail, industry, corporate and defined benefit funds are alternatives to SMSFs.

- ¤ SMSFs aren't for everyone and it's important to seek professional advice if you are considering setting one up.

CHAPTER 3

Setting up a self managed super fund

Get your facts first, then you can distort them as you please.
Mark Twain

If you have now decided to establish an SMSF, you will have a multitude of questions around how to establish the fund and what you need to do in order to move your superannuation assets from your current fund to your new SMSF. Once your assets have been rolled over into your SMSF, you will then need to know how to invest those assets on behalf of the fund while ensuring you are complying with SMSF rules.

> **Tip**
>
> If you need some help, go to my website at <www.samhenderson.com.au> for more information. My team can help you establish and administer your fund as well as provide financial planning and investment advice at fixed capped prices.

How easy is it to set up and run an SMSF?

SMSFs are easy to set up, and it generally costs less than a thousand dollars to do so. It's easy because you get someone else to do it for you. Don't do it yourself. A professional adviser, accountant or administrator will be far better placed to assist you and the cost is not prohibitive. Solicitors may also help construct the trust deed documentation, but they tend to be more expensive, more consultative and often have superfluous documents, but if your financial situation is complex, this may be a good option for you. Most of the professional web-based document providers that a specialist would use are in fact law firms that regularly update their documents. The websites for some of the companies that provide these services to professionals are <www.cleardocs.com.au>, <www.topdocs.com.au> and <www.superregistry.com.au>. There are many others, but your adviser will have their chosen provider for their own reasons.

If you are looking for a specialist adviser, try the SMSF Professional Association of Australia at <www.spaa.asn.au>.

Each fund needs to be registered with the ATO and have its own TFN (tax file number) and ABN (Australian business number). Again, your adviser will register you and should ensure that you have a tax agent registered to your fund so they receive all the tax notices from the ATO. You can do your own tax returns and administration except the audit, but I strongly discourage this unless you are a trained and up-to-date accountant, given the constant alterations to legislation.

While it's possible to do your own SMSF tax return, if you register with a tax agent you will have more time to prepare it, because you won't have to submit the return until May the following year. If you do your own return then it will be due at the end of October following the end of the financial year on 30 June. In your first year of submitting an SMSF return, however, the ATO does allow you to push that out until 28 or 29 February (assuming a leap year). The big issue arises when your investment tax reports do not come in from your investment providers if you own shares or managed funds until September or October and you then have to have your audit done, which may take another few weeks, so your chance of having a return in on time will be reduced. For these reasons, and the fact that you will probably need professional tax advice, I don't recommend doing your own tax return.

What will I call the fund?

A fund can be called anything you like and the name does not have to be unique, as the fund's TFN and ABN will be the fund's unique characteristics for the tax office to determine ownership. For example, there are probably thousands of Smith Family Super Funds. My clients have given their funds funny names such as the SKI Fund (which stands for Spend Kids' Inheritance), the Getoutoftown Fund or the Fatcat Fund, but most are simply given the surname of the family putting the fund together. My advice is to keep it short as you may be writing it many times in cheque books, share transfer papers or investment documents.

You will need to record the personal details of each of the proposed members for the trust deed establishment, including their TFN, place of birth and other details, to provide to the ATO. Your administrator will give you a form on which to record this information. You will then need to apply for a TFN and ABN with the tax office. Under the current system, it will take about 28 days for these numbers to be provided.

What is a trust deed?

A trust deed is a written document that describes how your SMSF will operate. It sets out the governing rules and regulations outlining how your fund is to be run and what it can and can't do. The trust deed's rules and regulations are subject to Australian law, and precedence is always given to Commonwealth legislation. Examples of some the issues that a trust deed addresses are as follows: who can be a member; how members can contribute to the fund; and how superannuation pensions will be paid in the future. It will also deal with issues such as creating new members, what happens on the death of a member and how the funds are to be invested, which will refer to a separate investment strategy.

A good trust deed needs to be flexible in its operations as to who can be a member, what investments can be considered and the many types of pensions that can be paid. It should allow for flexibility in superannuation laws and changes to those laws over time so you do not have to keep updating the deed each time the law changes. For example, in describing the types of retirement income streams, the trust deed may specify 'allocated pensions, account-based pensions, transition to retirement pensions or any other such pensions or income streams as allowed under superannuation legislation at the time'.

Trust deeds differ from provider to provider, so it's important to ensure that your chosen administrator, financial adviser or accountant has given some thought to your specific circumstances and made sure that the deed they use is suitable for your application. It is well worth reading through your trust deed to make sure you understand how your SMSF works. Most of them are easy to read, so don't be worried that your deed will be full of legal jargon.

> **Tip**
>
> Download a sample trust deed from <www.samhenderson.com.au> to see what one looks like and familiarise yourself with the contents.

What is a trustee?

A trustee is the person or group of people or company that is responsible for holding and managing the investments of the superannuation trust. In an SMSF each member is a trustee and each trustee is a member or director of the trustee company (if a company is the trustee), so the roles are interchangeable. A trustee has the onus of responsibility placed upon them to follow the superannuation laws of Australia and to protect the interests of other members of the fund managing their retirement benefits. Trustees must also follow the rules outlined in the trust deed, but Australian superannuation laws always supersede those of the trust deed in the event of an inconsistency.

Trustees of an SMSF must:

¤ act in the best interest of members when making decisions

¤ manage the fund separately from their own affairs

¤ ensure money in the fund is accessed only when the law allows it.

Despite the added levels of responsibility, nearly a million people have made the decision to become a trustee and take control of their superannuation and actively manage their own retirement savings.

Trustee declaration

The ATO has introduced the trustee declaration to make sure that you understand and acknowledge your obligations and duties as a trustee of an SMSF. A trustee declaration contains the following key acknowledgements:

¤   regulation of the fund by the ATO

¤   sole purpose test

¤   trustee duties

¤   your investment restrictions

¤   how the fund accepts contributions

¤   your administrative obligations

¤   your signature and acknowledgement.

Tip

Download a sample trustee declaration from <www.samhenderson.com.au>.

Types of structure for an SMSF

An SMSF can be set up under three types of structure:

¤   single-member fund run by two individual trustees

¤   a fund with two to four individual members and trustees

¤   a fund with one to four members run by a corporate trustee.

If you are single and want to establish an SMSF, you have two choices: you can establish your fund with yourself and one other individual trustee, preferably a relation who acts as a trustee but is not a member of the fund, or establish the fund with a corporate trustee — for example, ABC Pty Ltd as trustee for the Smith Family Super Fund. If you prefer to have your affairs completely private then I'd recommend using a corporate trustee, but if you are happy to share your affairs with a brother, sister or an adult child then it may be preferable to have them involved in the fund as an additional trustee. You can have also non-family members as trustees, but it may be preferable to keep things in the family.

The disadvantage of using a corporate trustee is that there are additional reporting obligations to be met, which do not have to be satisfied when individual members are fund trustees. For most mum and dad SMSFs, it is appropriate and cost effective to simply have two individual trustees who are also members but, if desired, you may have up to four members as individual trustees.

To use a corporate trustee to run your SMSF, you will have to register a company that becomes the trustee of the fund. All fund members must be directors of the trustee company so if a fund member needs to be replaced, you can change the directors, or if a fund member dies, the trustee company can be administered by external trustees or attorneys. This provides some flexibility from an estate planning perspective.

It will cost around $600 to $1000 to set up a company, depending on who establishes it for you. As directors of the corporate trustee, you will have further compliance obligations as different laws apply to companies than to superannuation trusts. For example, the ATO regulates SMSFs, but the Commonwealth *Corporations Act 2001* governs companies, which are regulated by the Australian Securities and Investments Commission (ASIC) so you will have two layers of regulatory obligations. Companies also have additional costs of around $300 a year for reporting purposes. Trustees and members therefore have to understand the corporations law as well as superannuation laws, which I feel is a disadvantage.

One advantage of having a company as a trustee is that banks require a corporate trustee if you want to borrow money to buy a property. Another reason for having a corporate trustee is that there is no time limit on the existence of a company, and it survives in perpetuity, unlike a trust, which has a life span of only 80 years. It is also easy to change directors if a member dies. However, I reckon it's easy enough to change members and trustees as individuals, without the additional overlay of a company structure.

If you are looking for simplicity, then a company structure is probably not for you. However, if you have significant assets (for instance, well over $1 to 2 million), or are considering borrowing to buy property or a highly diversified portfolio of shares, fixed interest, property or other more complex assets, then a company structure may be best for you. It's a good idea to talk to a professional and take their advice.

Who can be a member and a trustee?

The ATO's rules concerning SMSF trustees state the following:

¤ The trust must have four members or fewer.

¤ Each member must be a trustee.

¤ No member can be an employee of another member unless they are related.

¤ No trustee is to be paid for their services as a trustee.

¤ If a corporate trustee manages the fund, no director can be paid for their services as a director in their role as a trustee for managing the fund.

Individual trustees must meet further obligations to ensure that they are legally eligible to act as a trustee. They have to be aged over 18 (minors cannot be accepted as trustees), and they cannot be under a legal disability (for example, be of unsound mind). In addition, members cannot act as trustees if they:

¤ have been convicted of an offence involving dishonesty

¤ are subject to a civil penalty order under superannuation laws

¤ are insolvent

¤ are an undischarged bankrupt

¤ have previously been disqualified by a regulator such as APRA.

If a corporate trustee is running the fund, the directors cannot be disqualified persons, a liquidator must not have been appointed to the company, and an action to wind up the company must not have been commenced.

How many members will the fund have?

You can have up to four members in an SMSF. Members are typically individuals or husband and wife; adult children (over 18 only) may also be included in the fund. Unless the children have substantial assets in super, it may not be worth the additional cost and effort to maintain the fund with these extra members because of the extra administration, investment and accounts work required by additional members. Table 3.1 shows the proportion of number of members in SMSFs over the seven years to June 2010.

Table 3.1: percentage of number of members in SMSFs, 2003–10

Number of members	2003–04 %	2004–05 %	2005–06 %	2006–07 %	2007–08 %	2008–09 %	2009–10 %
1	20.8	20.7	20.6	20.9	23.7	23.1	22.6
2	67.9	68.2	68.7	68.9	67.1	67.9	68.8
3	5.6	5.5	5.3	5.1	4.6	4.5	4.2
4	5.6	5.5	5.4	5.1	4.7	4.6	4.0

Source: <www.ato.gov.au>.

What are binding nominations of beneficiaries?

When you establish your SMSF, the person or company setting it up for you will ask you whom you want to receive your assets in the event of your death. This is called nominating your beneficiaries. You can choose to make a binding nomination of beneficiaries to identify the dependants who will receive a lump sum or pension. The trustee must distribute your assets as you have specified. If you make a non-binding nomination, the trustee will take notice of your request, but can use his or her judgement in distributing your assets.

Dependants under superannuation law are different from dependants under tax law. Superannuation dependants can include;

¤   spouses (married, de facto, same sex)

¤   children (minor or independent adults)

- ¤ financial dependants or interdependants
- ¤ legal personal representatives of dependants.

As your SMSF is a trust, the assets fall outside the jurisdiction of your will and so need to be dealt with separately. The binding nomination identifies the party or parties to whom your assets will be distributed and in what percentages, for example, 50 per cent to my daughter Helen and 50 per cent to my son David (adult children are dependants under the SIS Act). The estate will be the default option but it is always best for beneficiaries to be able to immediately access funds or continue to receive pensions, in the event of a delayed probate or estate settlement process. Dependants always need cash flow so a binding nomination serves an important process.

While there is currently debate around the tax for beneficiaries receiving pensions and lump sums from a deceased member of an SMSF, cash flow is essential.

Binding nominations of beneficiaries need to be updated every three years as stated in the SIS Act. If personal circumstances change, such as marriage, divorce or children becoming independent, then those considerations need to be made when changing your binding nominations. You should also have a diary note or a mechanism to review your trust deed at least every three years for this reason. This also highlights the need for a trust deed to meet your lifestyle, life stage and estate planning needs.

If you die without a binding death nomination in place, the assets will fall under the jurisdiction of your deceased estate, but the assets will be subject to the probate process and the normal pace of probate, and any threats to the estate through appeals. This may slow down access to vital cash flow for beneficiaries against the intentions of the deceased. It's best practice to have an up-to-date and valid binding nomination of beneficiaries.

Opening a bank account

Once you have received your ABN and TFN from the tax office, you may then open a bank account or investment account in the name of your SMSF. The bank will need to see your trust deed, TFN, ABN and identification for trustees and signatories. Not everyone needs to be a signatory, but that is up to you and how you run your fund. I'd suggest opening a bank account independent of your share broker, accountant or financial adviser as you may need a cheque book to pay expenses, such as the $180 per year regulatory fee to the ATO to administer your fund (note that this fee is subject to change). You will also have accounting fees, advisory fees and other costs for which you will need a bank account.

Most importantly, the bank account in the name of the SMSF will be needed to receive superannuation rollovers from other institutions. It will be the central depository for your hard-earned superannuation savings before you start investing.

How to roll your funds over into your new SMSF

Rolling over your superannuation money from your existing super-annuation accounts is a simple process, but you will need to be organised. I suggest you follow this simple process.

1   Search for lost super on the ATO website <www.ato.gov.au>. Type SuperSeeker into the site's search function. When SuperSeeker opens you will need your TFN, name and date of birth to look for any super you have in accounts you have forgotten about. Another helpful website is <www.findmysuper.com.au>.

2   Once you have located all your superannuation funds, you should then call each super fund and ask for a rollover form. These may also be available on the fund's website.

3   In order to successfully roll over the funds, your present fund will need a completed and signed copy of its rollover form, specific forms of identification that have been certified as genuine copies of the original by a JP or equivalent, and a letter of compliance stating that your SMSF is a complying super fund in the eyes of the law. A sample letter of compliance can be found at <www.samhenderson.com.au>. The bank may also ask for the original confirmation letter from the ATO stating your ABN and TFN for your fund set-up. You should be able to find

details of the information your existing super fund needs to roll over your money and details about appropriate identification on the fund's website or call them to ask.

4   Your existing fund will also need the details of your SMSF bank account so they can deposit the funds directly or an address to which to send a cheque. All cheques will be made out to your SMSF, not your personal name. Remember, these are your super fund's assets, not your own personal assets and you may not access the funds until you meet a condition of release.

5   The rollover process may be slow but hopefully it will be completed in around two to three weeks. I'd suggest you make a nuisance of yourself and ensure that at each stage your existing fund has all the correct information at hand so they can execute a swift rollover.

Tip

Super funds don't like letting go of their money, even though it's really your money, so if they start asking for bank statements of your super fund then feel free to tell them that they are being too onerous and just to roll over your money — after all, it's your money not theirs!

Key points

☐   You need to find a trusted provider to help you establish your SMSF, such as a financial adviser, a specialist SMSF administrator or your accountant. Visit <www.samhenderson.com.au> if you need help finding someone.

☐   Make sure your trust deed is as flexible as possible concerning investments, types of pensions, nomination of beneficiaries and future changes to the law.

☐   You can call your fund anything you like, but keep it simple and memorable because you will be writing its name many times over the coming years.

☐   The three key SMSF structures are single-member funds with an individual or corporate trustee; a fund with two to four individual trustees, or a corporate trustee for one to four members.

¤ There are restrictions on who can be a member of a fund (see 'Who can be a member and a trustee' on p. 39) and how many members can be in a fund. The maximum number of members is four.

¤ An SMSF is run as a trust and its assets fall outside the jurisdiction of your will. A binding nomination of beneficiaries allows you to leave your superannuation assets to your chosen dependent beneficiaries.

¤ Make sure you or your provider sends your application for a TFN and ABN for your fund immediately to the ATO as it will take at least 28 days for them to provide the numbers once they receive your application. You may not be able to establish your SMSF's bank account or make your first investment in the SMSF or apply for roll over of your existing super money until you have these details.

CHAPTER 4

Running a compliant fund

The United States prefers that Iraq meet its obligations voluntarily, yet we are prepared for the alternative.

George W. Bush, former president of the United States

How does George W. Bush's comment relate to running an SMSF? It describes how the ATO thinks about SMSF trustees — and the tax office will certainly take action against you if you do not follow its rules in running your SMSF.

You would probably like to skip this chapter about what you should and shouldn't do with your retirement savings — after all, it's your money. But the reality is that it's not your money yet. It's not yours until you retire or meet another condition of release. That means this is probably the most important chapter of the book, because you need to understand these principals before investing a cent through an SMSF.

Overseeing a fund involves taking ownership of the compliance requirements to maintain the fund to an appropriate standard in the eyes of the ATO — the regulator of SMSFs. The responsibility of the fund's compliance rests with you, the member/trustee, not the tax agent, financial adviser or administrator that you use to complete the work.

You must understand the role and responsibilities of your position as a member/trustee of the fund, because if a problem is found, it is you that the ATO will penalise (see below for more on penalties for non-compliance).

Without fail, and before you set up an SMSF, download the following documents from <www.ato.gov.au>:

¤   *Thinking about SMSF*

¤   *Setting up a self-managed super fund*

¤   *Running a self-managed super fund.*

There are other booklets about regulation and winding up SMSFs that may be of interest, too, so have a look around while you are on the website.

What will happen when you get it wrong

Recently, the Deputy Commissioner of Taxation highlighted a case in which a trustee and member of an SMSF was penalised for gaining access to her superannuation money. While the member did not receive a custodial jail sentence, she gave the excuse to the ATO that she had to pay off her David Jones store card and she had dipped into her retirement savings accounts to reduce the debt.

Unfortunately for the trustee in this case, pleading ignorance was no defence and she was punished for her actions. As a trustee, you have obligations to diligently follow the letter of the law and any breaches of that law must be reported by you, your accountant or your auditor.

In another case, the trustee withdrew around $20 000 after he had set up his SMSF and rolled over his super funds into the SMSF. He consistently withdrew additional funds over several years for his personal use and even continued to withdraw money after receiving an audit notice from the ATO. In this case, he could hardly argue that the funds had been withdrawn by mistake and even ignorance could not be used as a defence here. The trustee was promptly fined $12 500 by the Federal Court and disqualified from acting as a trustee in the future.

In a third case, a member/trustee failed to complete tax returns properly for the fund for several years, and was given 10 months' weekend detention as a penalty. How extreme is that for not lodging your tax returns? Think twice before delaying your tax returns next year or, if you are a few years behind, bring them up to date immediately or you might be off to the slammer and walking the yard with hardened criminals.

Many of us don't like being told what to do when it comes to our money, but in the case of SMSF compliance it's a matter of comply or be penalised. Complex laws govern superannuation and, as with any non-compliance, ignorance is no defence. Each year, your auditor and your accountant will be required to sign off your accounts and they will not be willing to put their signature and their profession on the line for a non-complying fund. Penalties can be serious and there is plenty of evidence to suggest that the ATO is unwilling to compromise on even the most benign oversights, let alone deliberate efforts to flout the law.

Penalties for non-compliance

I'm sure you want to learn about more exciting things, like how to make a dollar in the sharemarket or purchase property in your super fund and put your retirement savings to work, but, as a motivation for not skipping through this chapter, it's appropriate to highlight the consequences of not running a compliant fund.

In the event that you or your other member/trustees break the rules of the *Superannuation Industry (Supervision) Act 1994* (SIS Act), the *Corporations Act 2001*, or the rules imposed by the ATO (such as the *Income Tax Assessment Act 1997*), or even the rules of your trust deed itself in running your SMSF, the potential penalties include:

- a fine of up to $220 000 for each breach, to be paid by the trustee personally (not by the SMSF)
- penalties, such as fund assets being taxed at 46.5 per cent instead of 15 per cent
- a jail sentence.

It should be noted that, in the event of a conflict between trust deed rules and the superannuation legislation, the legislation always takes precedence. Further, you will need to sign a trustee declaration within 21 days of commencing your fund. So, if you breach your obligations, the ATO has a signed document as evidence of your agreement to be a good member/trustee, which it can use against you in a court of law. The ATO doesn't miss a beat when it comes to compliance.

All that being said, remember that more than 400 000 Australians have taken on that responsibility of running a fund, and they are happily and compliantly running their own SMSF. In a recent year-end audit of around 6000 funds, the ATO identified around 185 of those as being non-compliant. So the percentage of non-compliance is very small (3 per cent of those audited). I just want you to understand the possible ramifications of non-compliance and the importance of following the rules.

Following the rules

Now that I've scared you into submission, you will need a firm grasp of the basic self managed superannuation investment rules. These rules constitute the fundamentals of investing for your SMSF so get to know them well and refer back to them before you do anything with your SMSF money such as buying, selling, transferring or investing your SMSF assets. I'll describe the five main rules first and then briefly outline other rules below.

The sole purpose test

The single most important of all the rules in managing an SMSF is satisfying the sole purpose test.

The sole purpose test dictates that the money and investments in your SMSF are for the sole purpose of providing retirement benefits to the fund's members and their beneficiaries. No member may receive a personal benefit from the fund until they meet a condition of release. Conditions of release include:

- retirement over age 55 (rising to 56 to 60 for people born after June 1960 to 1964)
- reaching age 65
- transition to retirement strategy
- financial hardship

⊠   disablement

⊠   funds less than $200

⊠   leaving Australia for good

⊠   death (not very practical for accessing superannuation).

Borrowing

Essentially, members may not borrow money inside the fund. This includes property investment loans and margin loans on investment assets in the fund. The theory behind this is that it creates uncertain risk for the assets within the fund and thus uncertain risk for hard-earned retirement dollars, and the government is less willing to help you fund your retirement if you are silly with your money.

You can invest in vehicles called warrants that allow you to borrow money inside your super fund, but the warrant structure has many rules and regulations designed to protect your retirement savings. See chapter 7 for more information on investing in warrants and how to use them to buy shares or property.

Borrowing is also allowed in limited circumstances: for up to seven days to settle security transactions, or for up to 90 days to make benefit payments to members. In either case, the amount borrowed may not to exceed 10 per cent of the fund balance, even for short-term borrowing.

Related party transactions

You cannot acquire assets in your SMSF from a related party of the fund. For example, your fund cannot buy a residential property owned by you personally (or held in joint names, a trust, or company that is related to you in any way).

However, transferring a commercial property is an exception to this rule. Business real property (as the ATO calls it) can be bought and transferred into an SMSF from your individual name or related entity. For many small business owners, their premises is part of their retire-ment strategy so the ATO recognises this and allows commercial property to be transferred into an SMSF. That being said, you can also transfer a commercial investment property that your small business does not reside in.

Importantly, residential properties cannot be transferred from a personal name to a superannuation fund — please commit this to memory, because it is one of the most common questions I am asked as a financial adviser and SMSF administrator.

Tip

Residential property cannot be transferred into an SMSF — but commercial property can.

As with all the rules of SMSFs, there are a limited number of exceptions to the related party transaction rules. Other exceptions include:

- The transfer of an asset (that is, a super contribution or a purchase by the fund from you personally) with a market value less than 5 per cent of the fund's total assets; for instance, your SMSF may purchase, invest, lease or lend up to 5 per cent of the fund's total assets held by a related party.

- The transfer of a business real property, which is property owned and controlled wholly and solely for the use of a business, not for investment purposes. If the property is partially leased, then a ruling or advice may be necessary to ascertain the inclusion of the full asset as business real property. An example might be where you run a business from the main premises and a granny flat at the back is leased as a residential-style investment.

The related parties of your fund are all associates of your fund, including members, their relatives (for example, spouse, children), business partners, employers or companies or trusts controlled by members, business partners, relatives or associates. In 2008, the definition of related party was widened to include same-sex partners.

In-house assets

According to the ATO, an in-house asset is an asset of the fund that is:

¤ a loan to a related party

¤ an investment in a related party or a related trust

¤ an asset of the fund subject to a lease or lease arrangement between a trustee of the fund and a related party of the fund.

As an exception, you may invest, lease or lend up to 5 per cent of the fund's balance to a related party.

The main exemption to the in-house assets rule is an investment in business real property. For example, when a small business owner wants to buy a building to operate their business from, they may purchase the building in the name of the SMSF and lease it back to the business. The theory is that many small business owners invest into their business (in preference to the standard superannuation structures) and that forms a large part of their retirement savings when they sell or exit the business to retire.

If you can't afford to put the property inside the super fund, there is a major added benefit to purchasing the business real property when the owner sells as they can exercise the principles of the capital gains tax exemptions for small business owners, which allows full or partial exemption from capital gains tax on the sale of the business goodwill and real property (see chapter 12 for more details).

The sale of a business real property asset inside the super fund at retirement is also free of capital gains tax (CGT). If you are not retired and your super fund is in accumulation mode, it will attract low rates of CGT: if the asset is held for more than 12 months and sold before retirement, it will attract 10 per cent CGT, and if it's held for less than 12 months it will attract 15 per cent CGT, same as the rest of the super fund's earnings.

If you are a small business owner who will have a saleable business at retirement, then make sure you read strategy 3 on page 193 — it will change the way you invest!

Arm's length transactions

The arm's length rule applies to all transactions in an SMSF. It exists to ensure that all transactions are undertaken on commercial terms. This may be one reason that residential property cannot be transferred from an individual's name to an SMSF, as there is a risk of owners undervaluing the transaction, which would result in a lower payment of stamp duty and reduced capital gains for tax purposes.

True commercial market value must be represented in all transactions completed by your fund. As you control your fund and your other assets, there may be a temptation to transfer assets at lower values into a fund to increase personal cash and increase the fund's assets. This temptation increases when share and property markets crash as individuals usually come under financial pressure and see their superannuation as a bucket of money to solve their short-term cash-flow problems.

The ATO is well aware of this temptation and many examples flowed from the recent GFC, when member/trustees accessed their superannuation funds, contravening the sole purpose test, or were tempted to transfer assets into their fund on non-commercial terms. So common was this temptation, that the ATO put out a booklet called, *Superannuation, It's Not Your Money Yet!*

All SMSF transactions need to be undertaken on commercial terms at arm's length unless you are completing a transaction that meets the exemptions listed above.

Other rules

Apart from the essential must know rules described above, there are a number of other rules that you must adhere to. Most of these are common sense. These rules include:

- securing your assets in the name of the fund or the trustee company
- acting honestly in matters concerning your fund
- exercising diligence and skill in managing your fund
- acting in the best interest of members

- ¤ separating the fund assets from the members' non-super money

- ¤ maintaining control of your fund (although you can outsource certain duties)

- ¤ allowing access to information for members

- ¤ following the superannuation rules.

Again, ultimate responsibility falls with the member/trustees of the fund, despite their ability to outsource some administrative tasks. This means that it is you that the ATO will penalise should the rules not be followed to the letter of the law.

What you need to do next

The good news is that help is readily available and maintaining a compliant fund is not particularly difficult if you know and understand the rules. The next steps you need to follow include the following:

- ¤ Write an investment strategy and keep it up to date.

- ¤ Keep regular minutes of meetings or fund decisions.

- ¤ Prepare annual accounts — statement of financial position (balance sheet), and statement of financial performance (also called the profit and loss statement or P&L).

- ¤ Prepare annual member statements.

- ¤ Conduct an annual audit.

- ¤ Prepare an annual tax return and statement of taxable income. Quarterly business activity statements (BAS) are also required for funds that have an annual turnover of $75 000 or more per year, excluding investment income. The vast majority of SMSFs won't need to do this, but those that earn commercial property income in excess of $75 000 will need to do a BAS. Check with your administrator if you are unsure.

- ¤ Pay your supervisory levy (currently $180 per year).

- ¤ Complete a trustee declaration within 21 days of fund establishment.

- ¤ Prepare an actuarial certificate if required.

In almost all cases, these activities can and should be outsourced to your service providers, such as accountants, financial advisers or specialist SMSF administrators. If this is your intention, then you must ensure that they actually complete all of these tasks competently and entirely. You may find your accountant is unwilling to write your investment strategy so you may need to do it yourself or see a financial adviser. The examples below will also help you if you haven't yet completed any of these documents.

Investment strategy

The first thing you will need once you have established your fund is a written investment strategy. I estimate that more than 30 to 40 per cent of funds do not have a compliant and up-to-date written investment strategy. The investment strategy allows you to document a method of investing the fund's money in a way that is appropriate to members. This means that the asset allocation and chosen products need to be implemented in a way that considers the members' attitudes to risk. Risk — the chance of losing money — is interpreted differently by different people and so member attitudes are a key consideration in the construction and implementation of the investment strategy.

Many people are happy to accept the theory of risk but they do not want to realise that risk in the form of tangible financial loss, but the two are one and the same — they are not mutually exclusive events or possibilities. Risk assessment and investing appropriately is extremely important and so is monitoring your investments. Changing the strategy may also be appropriate in different economic times. Keep in mind that you will never be expected to time markets or predict the future — no one has those powers nor does a piece of software or sharemarket or property newsletter.

A sample investment strategy follows. It is also available on my website at <www.samhenderson.com.au> for you to download and adapt for your fund. Alternatively, you should seek advice about ensuring your investment strategy is tailored to your fund's needs.

Investment strategy

For the Smith Family Super Fund

Investment objectives

The trustees of the above superannuation fund believe that the following general investment objectives should be considered:

- to provide superannuation benefits to the members of the fund to meet their retirement needs

- to ensure that an appropriate mix of assets are owned by the fund by taking into account the ages of the members

- to achieve a rate of return greater than CPI increases

- to maintain a low level of capital volatility

- to ensure that assets of the fund are liquid enough to meet expected cash-flow requirements

- to ensure that the fund has adequate diversification in the holding of its investments, including within classes of assets.

Investment strategy

To achieve the above investment objectives of the fund, the trustees have determined that the fund will consider investments in the following areas:

- equities and stocks including the participation in dividend reinvestment programs, rights issues and any other investments offered in this area

- listed property trusts

- unlisted property trusts

- other managed investments, including notes and debentures

- cash and any other interest-bearing deposits, including warrants.

The trustees of the fund also believe that to meet the investment objectives the following maximum and minimum investment levels should be considered.

(cont'd)

Investment strategy *(cont'd)*

Minimum and maximum investment levels for fund assets

	Investment levels %
Equities	40–70
Listed property trusts	0–10
Unlisted property trusts	0–10
Other managed investments	20–45
Cash	1–25

The trustees consider that a return of the CPI increase plus a further 3 per cent when averaged over a five-year period is a good return on investment.

In determining this strategy the trustees have considered all investment objectives, the fund's trust deed and any other relevant legislation.

It is noted that the trustees should also seek appropriate professional advice when required.

Policies

The policies of the fund are as follows:

- to continually monitor the performance of the fund's investments
- to monitor the liquidity requirements of the fund
- to monitor the economic and market conditions.

Source: <www.samhenderson.com.au>.

Record keeping and minutes

Record keeping is an important part of the maintenance of your SMSF. Most administrators will do all of this for you, but a word of warning: make sure you understand what level of service they provide and what things they do and don't complete for you, because the onus remains with you as the member/trustee. Finger-pointing and negligence are no excuse for non-compliance. The ATO likes to see consistent, accessible and accurate record keeping that provides an audit trail for the activity of your fund for a minimum of five years. This includes:

- an annual statement of financial performance (profit and loss)
- a statement of financial position (balance sheet)
- copies of annual returns submitted to the ATO for five years
- copies of other forms or statements lodged with the ATO.

You must keep the following records for a minimum of 10 years:

- minutes of meetings held with the trustees to record decisions affecting the funds
- records of changes in trustees
- copies of trustee declarations
- copies of members' written consent to be appointed as trustees of the fund
- copies of reports given to members (the ATO is a little ambiguous on this one, as the financial reports would be given to members).

In addition to the above, you have a legal obligation to:

- lodge an annual tax return for the fund
- pay the $180 annual SMSF supervisory levy to the ATO
- have an auditor complete an annual report (kept for 10 years).

Tax tip

Don't forget to complete a tax return for the fund for the year in which you establish the SMSF — even if there was no activity in the fund. For example, if the fund was established on 26 May, you will need to do a tax return for the tax year 26 May to 30 June, even if there were no transactions or money in your fund. The key here is to establish your fund shortly after 1 July in any tax year to avoid the unnecessary cost of a partial return on a fund that had no activity.

Minutes of meetings are an important and often overlooked essential part of ensuring accurate and consistent record keeping. To ensure you follow the stringent ATO guidelines, I have included a sample minutes of a meeting to adopt an investment strategy (from CPA Australia). You can you use this as a guide for future minutes of meetings that you have to record your funds decisions.

Sample Minutes of Meeting to Adopt Investment Strategy for SMSF

[Insert corporate trustee name [OR] individual trustee name(s)]

AS TRUSTEE FOR THE [insert name of Superannuation Fund] SUPERANNUATION FUND

MINUTES OF MEETING OF THE [insert name of Superannuation Fund] SUPERANNUATION FUND

HELD AT [insert address] ON THE [insert date, month, year]

PRESENT:	[insert the names of the directors of the trustee company OR the names of the individual trustees]
CHAIRPERSON:	Resolved that [insert name of appointed chairman of the meeting] be appointed chairperson of the meeting.
BUSINESS:	To discuss and formulate objectives and strategies and the investment plan for funds received for members.
OBJECTIVES:	Resolved that investment of members' funds be selected so as to give a return on investment at least equal to the current year CPI and in accordance with the attached memorandum [insert name of document containing the Investment Policy Objectives and Strategy].
STRATEGY:	Resolved that members' funds be so invested that on retirement dates of members the payments due on retirement may be made without affecting the objectives of the fund in accordance with the attached memorandum [insert name of document containing the Investment Policy Objectives and Strategy].

INVESTMENT PLAN:	Resolved that the attached memorandum **[insert name of document containing the Investment Policy Objectives and Strategy]** be adopted as a full range of available approved investment opportunities for members' funds as well as being an overview of investment policy, objectives and strategy.
CONFIRMATION:	Resolved that these minutes be accepted as a true and correct record of the proceedings in this meeting.

DATED the **[insert date]** day of **[insert month]**, **[insert year]**.

.... **[signed]**

Chairperson

Source: Reproduced with permission of CPA Australia.

Accounting

While it is quite possible to do your own accounting, in the same way that it is quite possible to do your own home renovations, I think this job is best left to the licensed professionals to ensure your legal obligations are met and the correct forms and notifications are submitted to the ATO. You will need to complete the following each year to keep your fund up to date:

- prepare annual accounts
- provide annual member statements
- conduct an annual audit
- submit an annual tax return
- pay your supervisory levy
- ensure new trustees complete a trustee declaration and submit it to the ATO
- obtain an actuarial certificate if that is appropriate for your fund.

Annual accounts

Your annual accounts are the statement of financial performance (formerly known as the profit and loss statement) and statement of financial position (formerly known as the balance sheet) for your SMSF. You will need to provide a tax report from your investment platform (if you have one), share transaction accounts, rental statements for property, bank statements for cash accounts and any other source documents that will provide your accountant with the necessary information to calculate your performance and track transactions.

Your accountant will also need the closing balances from the year before so if you have changed providers over the past year, the new accountant will need last year's tax returns. If you are a few years behind, then the accountant will need the last known tax return and to be able to rebuild your transactions. Don't panic if this happens, just fix it up. The worst thing you can do is to put your head in the sand and not bring your records up to date.

I have had clients who were five years behind in their tax returns and we have brought them up to date and into a compliant position. It will give you great peace of mind to be on top of your tax returns. You may have fines and interest to pay but that's much better than weekend detention at your local prison.

Annual member statements

The annual member statement shows the financial position of each member of the fund and records their individual contributions and withdrawals from the fund up to the end of each financial year, ending 30 June each year. Here are some examples of what will appear in each member's statement:

- member name and contact details
- member tax file number if it has been supplied
- date of birth
- date joined fund
- taxable and non-taxable components of balance

- preserved, non-preserved and unrestricted non-preserved parts of balance
- amount of concessional and non-concessional contributions over the past year (1 July to 30 June)
- income from the fund for the year
- any capital gains tax
- benefits, withdrawals or pensions paid from the fund
- contributions tax and income tax payable or refunded
- final member account balance for the year.

The member statement will state what components of superannuation make up the individual member's total benefit, or money, within the SMSF. For example, it will show that member one, as of 30 June, has $254 789 in their account, of which $204 789 is taxable and $50 000 is a non-taxable component. For member two, their statement might record a balance of $125 000, of which $100 000 is taxable and $25 000 is non-taxable.

The total in the fund in this case, assuming a two-person fund, may then be $379 789, and while the totals may be combined for investment purposes, each member will always retain their own member balances either on a percentage basis or because assets in the fund are segregated on the basis of ownership by different fund members. For example, one member may have shares to the value of $254 789 and the other member may have cash of $125 000. Alternatively, they could have $379 789 of shares and member one's percentage is 67 per cent and member two's percentage is 33 per cent. However, the annual member statement shows only the individual's details and not the details for the fund as a whole. The fund's total position is shown in the annual tax return, to which the member statement is attached.

> **Tip**
>
> For a sample financial statement that contains a member statement, see <www.samhenderson.com.au>.

Annual audit

Your annual audit will have to be carried out after your accounting statements have been completed and before your tax return is submitted to the ATO. The audit is completed by a third-party professionally licensed accountant who confirms the source documents are a true representation of what has actually happened throughout the year and that you have followed the rules and laws of managing your fund. The auditor should be an independent third party and best practice is to have someone from outside your accountant's business undertake the audit to ensure that it is truly independent.

The auditor's job is to assess the risk of the fund and confirm that the transactions recorded in the financial reports, including the statement of financial position and the statement of financial performance, actually occurred as reported. The auditor will also ensure that all *Superannuation Industry (Supervision) Act 1993* and other legal requirements are fulfilled and that the fund is a complying a fund.

More specifically, the auditor gathers evidence to support the financial statements, such as source documents. Their job includes testing some of the source document information to ensure it is a true and correct representation of what happened within the fund. For example, they will want to see a bank statement and follow a number of transactions to ensure they actually happened and all transactions were within the realms of superannuation law.

Not only will the auditor look at cash statements, share trading or property rental statements, but they will also assess contributions to and withdrawals from the fund to ensure that there have been no excess contributions or contravention of the conditions of superannuation release and other rules and laws. They will confirm the existence of the trust deed and that the rules set down in the trust deed have been followed.

Once the auditor has confirmed that the financial statements are, or are not, a true representation of the happenings in the SMSF, they will then prepare a report and document their findings. This is called the audit report. They keep a copy of that report for their own records and supply one for yours.

Tax returns

Once your accounts have been constructed and completed, income tax you owe the ATO or owed to you will be calculated, and the annual supervisory levy of $180 added or deducted. You must submit your fund's annual tax return once you have received your audit report. The tax return is much the same as the one you do for yourself each year, but it's for your fund and its members. If you pay too much tax in your fund, you will receive a refund and if you don't pay enough tax, then the fund may owe tax to the ATO. Your administrator or accountant will let you know where you stand.

Pay your supervisory levy (now $180 per year)

A supervisory levy of $180 is payable to the ATO each year as a regulatory fee. It is paid through your annual tax return.

Trustee declaration

The trustee declaration is simply where you as a trustee and each trustee signs off on the fact that the financial statements have been compiled in accordance with accounting standards, *Superannuation Industry (Supervision) Act 1993* and Regulations, and the trust deed of the fund.

Actuarial certificate if required for your fund

An actuarial certificate for the fund may be required to ascertain what income is taxable and what income is tax-exempt for account-based pensions, allocated pensions, defined benefit pensions or term-allocated pensions.

For example, one member may be in pension mode (drawing an income from the fund) and another member may be in accumulation mode (has not yet met a condition of release and is still working or is too young to access their super). The earnings of assets that support a pension are tax-free, so your accountant will need to ascertain what income from your assets is assessable and which income is exempt.

> **Tip**
>
> Incomes from member assets in account-based pension mode are exempt from income tax, capital gains tax and tax on earnings from investments. In fact, they are also eligible for a rebate of franking credits for company tax paid by the companies in which the fund owns shares. This is a major advantage of account-based pensions.

Where to get help

There are plenty of places to get help to run your fund, but make sure you engage a specialist in SMSFs by asking how many funds your provider administers. If it's fewer than 50, then they are not really a specialist. That being said, SMSFs are a diverse and new market, and no provider services more than 5000 funds out of a possible 400 000, so market share is very low and competition is very high — which is good for you, the consumer!

People who may help include:

- an accountant
- an SMSF specialist administrator
- a financial adviser.

From my experience, many financial advisers are poorly trained in SMSFs, although there is a group called the Self Managed Super Fund Specialist Advisers Association (SPAA). These people are well placed to understand SMSFs. Internet-based administrators do not provide a personalised service, so I suggest your accountant or a specialist administrator will be better placed to fulfil your needs. Establishing a relationship with someone you can talk to and get advice from will be very helpful.

> **Tip**
>
> Check <www.samhenderson.com.au> for a list of recommended SMSF providers and how to find a good one.

Key points

¤ Download these two documents free from <www.ato.gov.au> or <www.samhenderson.com.au>: *Thinking about Setting up an SMSF*, and *Running a Self Managed Super Fund*, which discusses your roles and responsibilities as a trustee (this is the preferred booklet and information source).

¤ The sole purpose of superannuation and superannuation funds is for retirement planning purposes only — you must not receive a personal benefit from running an SMSF until a condition of release has been met.

¤ In making investments, your fund must:

■ avoid borrowing, unless through investing in warrants or the borrowed money represents less than 5 per cent of fund assets

■ avoid related party transactions

■ undertake transactions on an arm's length, commercial basis

■ avoid investing in in-house assets.

¤ Each year you must review, update or complete the following documents:

■ trust deed

■ binding nomination of beneficiaries forms

■ investment strategy

■ financial statements including member statements; statement of financial position; statement of financial performance; tax return; supervisory levy; trustees declaration; actuarial certificate (if required by the circumstances of your fund).

Tip

A host of administrators out there are willing to help your SMSF. If you get confused or need a recommendation visit <www.samhenderson.com.au> to get help.

Types of investment

Many different types of investment are available for your SMSF. One of the most difficult decisions you will face when managing your portfolio is which assets to buy and sell, and in what proportions. In this chapter we will look at the various asset classes that you might consider when constructing the investment strategy for your SMSF: cash, fixed interest, shares, property and derivatives.

Income and growth

There are two reasons we want to buy assets for investment: income and growth. The sum of these two attributes equals your total return. The conundrum is that each asset class attracts different rates of return over time. Cash is relatively stable but barely keeps up with inflation, though it will provide an income, and shares can be volatile but have good long-term returns (growth) as well as providing cost-effective income. It is your job as the trustee to seek the combination of asset classes that best fit the personalities and attitudes towards risk of the members of your SMSF (see chapter 6).

Cash

Cash is king! Cash is literally money sitting in the bank in either an account that is readily accessible any day of the week or a term deposit. Cash offers no capital growth and is virtually risk-free. Cash allows to you take up opportunities when they arise so it's always a good idea to have at least 5 to 20 per cent of your portfolio in liquid cash. If your SMSF is in pension mode, then I would suggest a higher cash amount to ensure you have some both for investment opportunities and plenty to pay pensions for members. You probably need about enough cash to pay two years' worth of pensions, allowing also for the payment of dividends from shares. (SMSFs with pensions should never reinvest dividends when income is needed to pay pensions.) That being said, term deposits will also help to increase returns, so having all the cash liquid, or immediately available, may not be entirely necessary.

Cash used to be simply cash in the bank, but these days cash is a product touted by all the banks who are hungry for internal funding. Many banks offer cash accounts that have honeymoon periods of high interest rates, which fall 2 per cent a year after six months, or they offer term deposits of varying periods with varying rates. Some banks want short-term money, while others want longer term funds so they offer better rates over the longer term.

Shop around for the best cash deals and don't simply accept your bank's standard offers. Many banks will negotiate on cash rates and term deposits, much as they do on home loans, so do your homework and put some pressure on your bank to match the best rates around. The more cash you have, the more negotiating power you will have. For amounts over $500 000 or $1 million, the banks will bend over backwards to get your business.

I classify term deposits as liquid cash because most banks will allow you to break the term if you forgo the interest, so you can access your money if necessary, but it's also possible to classify term deposits as fixed interest investments, as they compete for the same space as bonds, although I think that bonds have an additional capital risk that term deposits don't have, which is why I distinguish between the two.

Term deposits are available for all terms, including 1, 3, 6, 9, 12, 24, 36, 48 and 60 months (five years). It's a good idea to take out a series of different rolling term deposits so your cash matures at different times, diversifying your cash exposure and income to factor in possible opportunities as they arise in riskier asset classes or to provide liquidity for your portfolio.

The importance of liquidity is often underestimated in portfolio management, but since the GFC, liquidity has become one of the most important factors to be considered in investing. Cash provides the vital liquidity when volatility strikes, and you don't want to crystallise losses if you don't have to. Losses are only paper losses until you actually sell an asset and realise that loss. When markets turn negative — and you can be sure they will — it is often the best time to buy good companies at good prices. I often take a contrary view in times of volatility, which means that I am often buying when others are selling and news is bad. Remember, cash is king!

Risk management

Your job as a trustee is avoiding bad investments as much as picking successful ones. One bad investment can cost you dearly, so do your homework or get an adviser you can trust.

Fixed interest

Fixed interest investments, such as bonds, can be a complex area of investment and so most SMSFs in Australia have tended to invest in cash, Australian shares and a little property. Bonds are like lending money to the government or a company and receiving a rate of interest for a period of time until your money is returned to you. The higher the risk — based on the likelihood of receiving your investment back — the higher the interest rate. Bonds are rated on risk and just because an investment is in a bond it does not necessarily make it safe. In recent years, however, bonds have taken off in popularity as interest in shares and managed funds has waned, partly because of sharemarket uncertainty caused by the GFC and the European debt crisis.

Several different types of bonds are available. Some are available only through their issuers, while many others can be traded on the ASX. Examples of bonds include:

¤ federal government bonds

¤ state government bonds

¤ utility bonds

¤ corporate bonds

¤ hybrids.

Federal and state government bonds are fairly simple products, as they have a predetermined time frame and usually a fixed rate of interest (known as a coupon rate) paid at regular intervals until maturity. At maturity, you get back the lump sum you invested. Utility bonds are just like state government bonds, but they are backed by the utility company, such as a power or water company. Most government bonds are not available to retail investors like you and me; they are only available to institutions or available through managed funds or exchange traded funds (which are like managed funds, but traded on the sharemarket). In 2011, the New South Wales government announced a bond issue to the public — the media dubbed them 'Barry Bonds' after Premier Barry O'Farrell.

Corporate bonds are bonds offered by corporations. Some are listed on the ASX and some are not, but, like all bonds, they are only as good as the company issuing them. During the GFC a number of companies that had offered bonds went into liquidation, taking investors' money with them, exposing SMSFs to losses in an area previously thought to be safe. As such, corporate bonds are significantly riskier than government bonds and so they pay higher rates of interest. Many corporate bonds have similar attributes to government bonds, where they pay a fixed rate of interest for a predetermined period, often five years, and then return your capital when the investment matures.

Recent years have seen the emergence of hybrid securities. Hybrid securities are corporate bonds that generally pay quarterly or half-yearly rates of interest on your investment, but the way the interest is paid may vary; for instance, the payment may be franked or not. Similarly, the final result at maturity may include a repayment of your capital, a rollover into a new bond, an increased rate of return if the company needs your money longer (called a step-up premium) or your investment may be turned into ordinary listed shares in the company. Because of the number of variables involved, these securities have been called hybrids because they aren't purely bonds.

There are fixed rate hybrids and floating rate hybrids. Like a government bond, a fixed rate hybrid will have a fixed rate of return until maturity. A floating rate will have a predetermined rate above the current Reserve Bank of Australia (RBA) cash rate or the bank bill swap rate. For example, consider a Commonwealth Bank–issued hybrid security that is listed on the ASX under the five-letter code CBAPA. CBAPA pays a fully franked dividend 3.4 per cent above the RBA cash rate. So if the RBA cash rate is 4.5 per cent and CBAPA is paying a premium, you will receive 4.5 per cent plus 3.4 per cent = 7.9 per cent return on your investment. If the RBA lowers rates, then your rate of interest will drop in line with the RBA move. If the RBA raises rates, your interest will increase in line with the RBA move.

All bond prices are very sensitive to interest rate moves. Fixed rate bonds increase in price when interest rates go down because the return on new bonds will be lower, making the higher rate fixed rate bonds more attractive to investors, so their capital value increases. Floating rate bonds, like hybrids, increase in value in a rising interest rate market. If you are going to invest in bonds, it's important to understand the effects of interest rates on your investment.

If you are going to invest into hybrids, then you should read the original product disclosure statements (PDSs) closely to understand how the product works, what the risks are and how the product will react to changing financial markets.

Tip

For more information on fixed interest products, such as bonds or hybrids, have a look at <www.fiig.com.au> (owned by FIIG Securities Limited, a specialist in fixed interest investments). To compare term deposits (and other rates and products) go to <www.canstar.com.au> (owned by CANSTAR which rates fixed interest and financial products, such as term deposits and mortgages) or <www.ratecity.com.au> (which also compares various financial products such as term deposits, credit cards and mortgages and is powered by CANSTAR).

Shares

Shares are small units of ownership in companies listed on the ASX. Each unit represents a small part of equity, or ownership, in that company. Each of the entities listed on the ASX has a certain number of shares on issue, and the total value of all those shares equals the market capitalisation (also called market cap), or the market value, of the company. The price of those shares varies from company to company and so the value of a 20c share can not be compared with that of a $50 share, as the value of an individual share depends on the company's market value, how much of its equity is listed and how many shares are on offer, to name just a few of the variants affecting pricing. Some companies don't list all of their equity and can have unlisted shares owned by founding shareholders or executives.

The ASX provides the ability to buy and sell shares, which in turn provides liquidity (the ability to turn your investment into cash in a speedy and efficient fashion). Liquidity is really important and is the primary reason that listed shares in companies sell for higher earnings multiples than unlisted shares. For example, I can't readily sell small parcels of shares in my company because it is a private and not a public company, and there is no exchange to allow me to sell. I would have to hire a business broker and put the sale out to tender, which could take months or years. Companies listed on the ASX therefore have a mechanism for traders to buy and sell small portions of their equity, called shares. The added liquidity afforded to ASX-listed company shares allows them to sell for five to more than 20 times earnings (profit), or even more, whereas shares in private, unlisted companies sell for between one and eight times earnings depending on such things as their growth, industry, cash flow, profitability and market share.

Liquidity, while providing easy access to cash, also facilitates volatility in share prices as people are continually buying and selling. Volatility also occurs on less liquid, small cap (low value capitalisation) stocks because there are not always buyers matching sellers' prices, so we may see large fluctuations in price that may not represent the true value of a company's shares. It's much easier to value a large, liquid company than a smaller company, because the larger company's shares are traded more readily. Pricing inconsistencies in listed companies allow investors to take advantage of opportunities in mispricings and buy good companies at lower than expected prices, with the prospect of capital growth. Share prices are simply a matter of supply and demand.

Benjamin Graham's Mr Market story

In his famous book *The Intelligent Investor*, first published in 1949 and described by Warren Buffett as 'the best book about investment ever written', Benjamin Graham illustrates the irrational behaviour of the sharemarket by describing a fictional character called Mr Market. The story goes something like this.

Mr Market is an investor who offers to buy and sell your shares at a different price every day depending on his mood, which can range from very optimistic to highly pessimistic. His moods vary wildly. The prices he suggests can sometimes represent the exact price of a stock, but more often than not he is not a good valuer of company share prices because he is very emotional.

It's therefore up to the investor to take advantage of the situation when shares are undervalued by having a method to value shares and identify opportunities when they arise.

The global sharemarkets are very similar to Mr Market's moods. Share prices swing from wildly cheap to wildly expensive, depending on the mood of investors and not necessarily because investors fairly value shares every day. The sharemarket is inefficient and often provides great opportunities for savvy investors to buy good companies at low prices. The strategy, in Warren Buffett's words, is to 'be greedy when others are fearful and fearful when others are greedy'. Benjamin Graham describes the situation as providing an opportunity to buy wisely when prices fall sharply and to sell wisely when they advance a great deal.

Before you decide to invest in a company, you need to know that its policy of distributing its earnings matches the investment objectives of your SMSF and its members. Companies that distribute all their earnings will have nothing to reinvest back into their business to provide growth. For example, many listed property companies distribute all of the profit back to their investors. But BHP, as a different example, distributes a small amount back to investors: it pays a dividend of about 2.5 per cent of the value of the company, which represents just 21 per cent of its annual profit. The remaining 79 per cent of the profit is reinvested into the company, allowing it to grow through acquisition or organic growth. Banks tend to distribute around 70 per cent of their earnings to investors and reinvest about 30 per cent into the business, providing investors with a combination of income and growth from their shares. Australian banks pay dividends of around 6 per cent of the share price, which means they are both growth and income focused which is why, when combined with other factors such as good management, a lack of competition and high barriers to entry, they can make good long-term investments if economic conditions allow.

The key reasons for SMSFs to own shares are capital growth, dividend payments and liquidity. The difficulty is in choosing the right shares to give you an optimum level of each of these three attributes to help you meet your investment objectives. Further, you will need to include some other asset classes to augment your investment strategy.

Full-service brokers versus online share broking

You can directly trade shares in two ways:

¤   through a full-service broker

¤   through an online broker.

A full-service broker will generally provide you with research specific to your situation and individual stock recommendations to help you establish and manage a share portfolio. Ideally they will pro-actively manage your portfolio over time and make changes to your portfolio when needed. Of course, this doesn't always happen and given that brokers make their money out of trading, they may make recommendations that increase their turnover and revenue. Expect to pay around 0.5 to 1 per cent of the total value of your investments managed by a broker per year for a full-service broker.

Full-service brokers usually provide services such as newsletters and research reports that they send out to clients, and these may be valuable in helping you in the investment decision-making process. The newsletters may also develop your understanding of the sharemarket and how companies are valued on the stock exchange. Newsletters will also discuss economic and political issues, and other influences on the sharemarket, which will also increase your understanding of how share prices work.

If you decide to use a full-service broker, make sure they are experienced, licensed and well educated on the companies they are recommending. Don't go with a young and inexperienced broker who just follows the company recommendations blindly. You want someone who is well engaged in their job and has seen tough times as well as good.

Online brokers are really transactional only and Comsec (owned by Commonwealth Bank) owns the lion's share of the market in Australia. E*TRADE and Bell Direct are other popular platforms, and most of the banks also have their own trading platforms too. Comsec and E*TRADE have good research available and offer reasonable analysis on most listed companies, but the information and recommendations may be out of date, so don't necessarily rely only on all the information you see.

Augment your online trading platform with a good newsletter or research house to keep you up to date with the latest recommendations and economic information. The banks also distribute their economic views and you can often pick up their free reports from their websites (for example, Westpac's weekly economic update). They are a good read and will familiarise you with economic research.

Online brokers charge anything between $15 and $50 to place a trade, but they may charge more for international trades and large value trades. They are definitely cheaper than full-service brokers but, of course, do not offer advice. It's really up to you as to whether you need or want advice, and what level of advice you feel is appropriate for the management of your SMSF. For example, if you just want to buy a group of blue-chip shares and hold onto them for the long term, then you may not need advice at all.

Researching shares

At Henderson Maxwell we use a plethora of share research to help us make decisions about our clients' money. Some reputable research tools that may help you include:

¤ the DIY Investor website <www.thediyinvestor.com.au>

¤ Alan Kohler's *Eureka Report* <www.eurekareport.com.au>

¤ *The Economist* magazine <www.economist.com>

¤ *Australian Financial Review* <www.afr.com>

¤   software research companies such as Lincoln Indicators <www.lincolnindicators.com.au) or Clime <www.clime.com.au>

¤   *farrelly's* <www.farrelly.com.au>

¤   a share-based newsletter like Fat Prophets <www.fatprophets.com.au> or Morningstar <www.morningstar.com.au>

¤   *Stock broker* newsletters from UBS or Macquarie

¤   world sharemarket information, *FTSE All-World Review*

¤   ETF research, *Pennywise* <www.pennywiseinvestment.com.au>

¤   your online broker, such as E*TRADE <www.etrade.com.au> or Comsec <www.comsec.com.au>

¤   economic research <www.anz.com.au> or <www.westpac.com.au>.

Magazines such as *Smart Investor* <www.afrsmartinvestor.com>, *Australian Property Investor* <www.apimagazine.com.au> or *Money* magazine <www. finance.ninemsn.com.au/money-mag> are also very useful research tools.

We obtain different research for different reasons. It's important to select the right tool for the right job. We use the banks' economic updates to shed light on economics; farrelly's for asset allocation and market sector valuations; and Morningstar, Fat Prophets, Lincoln and our own valuation tools for stock valuation. Each tool or source of information has a different application to help us find the right mix and ratio of stocks for a share portfolio. We also undertake research for term deposits and bonds, and then go directly to the providers to get the best deal for clients. In managing your SMSF, you need to develop your individual approach to get the best result you can achieve for your fund.

Share investment can be tricky and many people exit shares right at the time when they should be buying more. More often than not, most people's first experience in shares could be likened to gambling because they buy a stock or two, usually a two-bit start-up, tech stock, bio-tech or resource company that was recommended by a friend, wait for it to go down and then sell at loss. They then tell their friends how bad share investing is and try their hand at property, usually with a similar result.

As Warren Buffett says, 'A rising tide lifts all boats but it's not until the tide goes out that we realise who's swimming naked'. This rings true for the property industry as much as sharemarkets — we have discovered in the past few years that neither share nor property markets always go up in value. Research is essential and having a method of pricing assets to allow you to make good decisions is so important.

Types of shares and share activity appropriate to SMSFs

Given you have an obligation under the sole purpose test to manage your SMSF for the primary purpose of providing retirement benefits to members, it is prudent to take a conservative approach to managing your money. Appropriately, I would suggest for the average SMSF a portfolio of around 15 to 20 stocks of mainly blue-chip, top fifty ASX 200 companies. If you have more than $2 or 3 million in your super fund, then it may be appropriate to have a little more diversification, perhaps up to 25 to 35 stocks, but 35 would be at the upper end of the scale. Many fund managers have fewer than 30 stocks in hundred million dollar portfolios.

Try to keep small holdings to a minimum to reduce the paperwork caused by corporate actions (buy-outs, rights issues, takeovers, share splits, for instance). Since your shares will one day have to fund your retirement, income-based stocks are always good. Keep in mind that, because you pay just 15 per cent tax on investment income inside superannuation, a stock that pays fully franked dividends will give the fund a 15 per cent tax rebate from the tax office, which will increase your income. In pension mode, this rebate will be 100 per cent of franking credits because your investments will be completely free of investment earnings tax (and capital gains tax) inside a pension structure, which may add another 1.5 per cent to your portfolio value in income each year.

Franking credits

Franking refers to the level of tax a company has paid on the dividend it pays you; company tax is currently 30 per cent. If your dividend is described as fully franked, then the company has paid all 30 per cent tax on that dividend on your behalf. You do not have to pay any further tax on that dividend if your tax rate is 30 per cent. If your tax rate is 45 per cent, then you will have to pay an additional 15 per cent tax. However, if your tax rate is less than 30 per cent, as in the superannuation system where you pay just 15 per cent earnings tax in accumulation mode or zero tax in pension mode, you will receive a refund at tax time for your SMSF. Franking credits are designed to ensure that dividends aren't double taxed. Note that some shares have only 50 per cent franking and others vary from 0 per cent to 100 per cent franking. If you own shares now, perhaps you could have a look and check what levels of franking your current shares have.

Here's how you calculate the value of a franking credit. Let's take Commonwealth Bank shares as an example. Assume Commonwealth Bank shares are trading at $50 and paying a 5.7 per cent dividend that is fully franked. To determine what your pre-tax dividend is, we use the following equation.

$$\text{Pre-tax dividend} = \frac{\text{dividend}}{(1 - (\text{percentage franking} \times \text{company tax rate}))}$$

Now let's add the numbers:

Dividend = 5.7 per cent
Franking = 100 per cent
Company tax rate = 30 per cent

So for our CBA example:

$$\frac{5.7 \text{ per cent}}{(1 - (100 \text{ per cent} - 30 \text{ per cent}))}$$

= 8.14 per cent

Transferring shares into super—technical tips

Unfortunately, in late 2011 the government proposed that, by July 2012, transferring shares into your superannuation fund would be outlawed. Until July 2012 it will still be possible to transfer shares into your SMSF. In the event that you will have time to transfer shares, you may transfer shares from your own name, joint names or a partner's name into super, but the transfer is deemed to be a disposal for capital gains tax in the name of the share owner or owners.

Although you can do an in-specie transfer (transfer the shares themselves without selling them, which is an off-market transfer) of your shares, the ATO's view is that you have effectively sold the share in your own name and acquired it in the name of the super fund, so you will have a capital gains tax liability, assuming the share has increased in value since you bought it, and also assuming it is an asset bought after 20 September 1985. (Assets bought before 20 September 1985 are free of capital gains tax.)

In the same way, you could create a capital loss, which can be offset against any capital gains. If you are planning to transfer a portfolio of shares where some have gains and some have losses, you are can use the difference to try to manage your capital gains situation in a way that minimises your tax liability.

Share transfers can be treated as a concessional contribution or a non-concessional contribution, but you cannot transfer shares out of the super fund as a pension payment, because all pension payments must be made in cash. You can transfer shares out of the fund as a lump sum withdrawal; however, for people over the age of 60 and retired, this transfer out of the fund can be done free of tax. You need to meet all the normal contribution, withdrawal and conditions of release laws when considering transferring shares or even cash into or out of superannuation.

Also, keep in mind that these laws are in the process of change and to check with your adviser or broker about this proposed change, and the effects on your particular financial situation, as they had not gone through parliament at the time of writing.

For more on share investment and analysis, read the section on shares in my first book, *Financial Planning DIY Guide*.

Advantages and disadvantages of owning shares in your SMSF

There are several advantages to owning shares inside your super fund:

- ¤ Shares can provide good income for super funds.
- ¤ Shares have low maintenance costs: you don't have to pay strata fees as you would if you owned property in a strata scheme.
- ¤ Shares have low transaction costs: you pay no stamp duty when you buy or sell them.

⌘   You can borrow money to buy shares through a warrant structure, much as you can with property.

⌘   You can sell shares free of capital gains tax when you retire.

⌘   You may be able to transfer shares into or out of your super fund depending on proposed changes and the date of implementation.

⌘   Shares are highly liquid and easy to trade.

There are several disadvantages to owning shares inside your super fund:

⌘   Shares can be volatile and risky.

⌘   You need good research to choose the right stocks to invest in.

⌘   Some people find shares hard to understand and research difficult to read owing to the jargon surrounding share investment.

⌘   Many people speculate in risky shares rather than buying blue-chips.

Property

I often say, 'property for wealth creation and shares for wealth management'. The reason for this is that shares produce better after-tax income without the costs of maintaining direct property. In addition, many people use the tax benefits afforded to property investors to build their property portfolios by using tax-deductible debt to finance purchases. But in retirement, you no longer have a taxed income, so the benefits of borrowing money to invest are negated.

Changes to superannuation law introduced in 2007 allow a person to borrow money inside their super fund, so for most people, it makes more sense to buy property inside super than outside of super. Most people haven't worked this out yet or they simply don't have enough money in their super fund to justify a property purchase and the establishment of an SMSF (see chapter 7 for more information on this). However, you can effectively purchase the property inside your fund, pay it off with tax-effective superannuation contributions (9 per cent superannuation guarantee or salary sacrifice) and then sell the property at retirement free of capital gains tax.

There are many ways to own property inside your super fund. The most popular method has been through property security managed funds, which are managed funds that own commercial property syndicates and listed commercial property companies. These types of funds were hammered in the post-GFC environment and many frozen managed funds turned people off investing in commercial property, so there has been a movement away from listed property and into direct property.

Listed commercial property does have a few advantages that direct investment properties do not have. One of the key benefits is liquidity. Because the companies are listed on the ASX, shares in them can be sold almost instantly, so you will receive your cash quickly, whereas direct properties sit on the market for at least four to six weeks while an agent advertises the property for you, and then it will take another four to six weeks to settle the property once it is sold. So it will take around three months on average to realise the value of your investment in cash.

Many listed commercial property companies produce high dividends that have already accounted for strata fees, maintenance, agents' fees, land tax, stamp duty and all the other direct costs that you are responsible for as a direct property owner. Often when a direct property investor adds up all the costs of maintaining their property investment, they are left with little more than an investment return of 3 per cent or less on their investment. For retirees, this is not enough income to live on, so the risk taken is not justified by the income received. The opportunity cost of owning the property is not justified — opportunity cost is the dollar difference between taking one course action versus another more ideal course of action.

The two main types of direct property are commercial and residential. Small business owners have been able to build their asset bases in commercial property by owning the property that their business occupies inside their super fund. For many small business owners, this will be their nest egg for retirement.

In concert with the ability to own commercial property inside your super fund, the ATO also permits small businesses capital gains tax exemptions if the assets are held outside the super fund, allowing small business owners to sell their commercial property, business assets and goodwill free of capital gains tax if the assets are less than a combined $6 million in value, and up to $1.2 million can then be contributed to the super fund. The money does not have to go into super to attract the tax concessions but there are number of uses to maximise the benefits using superannuation. (This strategy will be explained in more detail in chapter 12 as it is a little complex and needs to be understood in its entirety if you are a small business owner. Don't skip chapter 12 if you are a small business owner, because it could save you hundreds of thousands of dollars in tax.)

Tip

You should also see the ATO website for more information about the small business CGT concessions (type 'small business CGT concessions' into the search box at <www.ato.gov.au>).

According to the latest figures from the ATO regarding the asset allocation of SMSFs, direct residential investment property currently makes up less than 4 per cent of the value of all money held in SMSFs, yet it is said that 20 per cent of the population own investment properties outside of their superannuation, that is, in their own names. I'm sure the popularity of superannuation as a property investment vehicle will increase significantly over the next few years as SMSF popularity itself continues to grow.

If you are thinking about buying a property in your SMSF, there are many factors to consider and, as with shares, you need to do your research. It's important to understand the factors affecting the area in which you are considering buying, the demand from other buyers and especially the demand from potential tenants who are going to give you your income stream for many years to come. A number of research houses, such as RP Data and Residex, provide individual property and suburb reports that will help you make the right decision about which property to purchase.

Tip

When researching properties consider using one of these companies to help you make better decisions: RP Data <www.rpdata.com.au> and Residex <www.residex.com.au>.

If you are planning to buy a strata unit, make sure you read the minutes of the building's committee meetings over past few years so you understand the situation with regards to the owners' corporation or body corporate raising money, which will affect your potential future costs. Also make sure you understand how the owners' corporation or body corporate fees will affect your after-cost yield on the investment. Strata costs can vary enormously. If you are an investor, don't become enamoured of pools, lifts and fancy common areas, because they can cost you a fortune in maintenance fees.

No matter which investment property you buy, make sure you have a depreciation schedule that allows you to depreciate both the building and fittings and fixtures within the building. Many companies can do this for you and most will guarantee to save you their fee in the first year or the service is free. It's a risk-free way to gain better cash flow. Depreciation allows you to claim the falling value of the building as an annual expense, so you can thereby claim a greater tax deduction on the property. While the value of the building is falling, hopefully the value of the land is increasing. The important point to make is that a depreciation schedule helps your after-tax cash flow because, while you can claim depreciation as an expense, it doesn't actually require you to put your hand in your pocket and pay the expense. I call it a non-cash cash-flow benefit. This may sound a bit confusing but check out the websites in the accompanying tip to find out more.

Tip

Companies that can help you create a depreciation schedule include Depreciator <www.depreciator.com.au>, Depro <www.depro.com.au> and Washington Brown <www.washingtonbrown.com.au>.

Fundamental to the property purchase is understanding your cash flow. Too many people buy property on the premise that it will simply go up in value. Not all properties go up in value and there is nothing worse than having a property investment that doesn't rise in value and also has negative cash flow. That's called a liability and not an investment, so research is really important and you should have a look at different areas and property types before you buy.

Many of the property investment magazines have stories and tips on where to buy and what to look out for. They also provide statistics on growth rates and vacancy rates that can be helpful. Perhaps consider subscribing to a few before making your decision to buy property inside your SMSF. Just make sure you avoid the spruikers and scammers, as those otherwise useful magazines are full of advertisements by people wanting to make huge commissions by selling you a property or offering their services. Beware and be aware of the property industry from that perspective as it is often better to buy a property directly than through a company selling properties as many receive 5 per cent commission for selling you a property in an area that will never flourish.

There are two reasons to buy property: for income and capital growth. If you are buying for your SMSF, you should be aiming for good income and solid growth over the long term. You may need to refer to your written investment strategy and make changes to it if you are going to use a large portion of your fund as a deposit for a property or to buy a property outright. Once you have made changes to your investment strategy, you then need to make sure that the property purchase is suitable for your SMSF from both an income and growth perspective.

The key to ensuring you make a good decision on behalf of your SMSF is by understanding your cash flows and doing your research. Combine this with an understanding of how your superannuation contributions are going to boost your super fund's balance to repay loans, if you borrow money, or to boost your superannuation, allowing it to gain greater diversity through investment in other asset classes as your non-property balance increases. This will affect your future investment decision making.

Advantages and disadvantages of owning property in your SMSF

There are several advantages to owning property inside your super fund including:

- the ability to borrow money to pay for the property
- the ability to pay off a property faster inside super than outside super, because of tax-effective super contributions

- no capital gains tax liability if the property is sold after you retire

- the fact that the property will probably be cash-flow positive because you need a larger deposit if investing through an SMSF.

There are also some disadvantages to owning property inside super including:

- borrowed money can't be used to develop, renovate or improve the property

- the profits from the property can't be accessed until you meet a condition of release

- property structures needed to operate under the warrant structure required to borrow money in your SMSF can be expensive to set up

- money borrowed inside super usually attracts higher interest rates

- a higher deposit is needed (usually at least 30 per cent) to buy property in your SMSF

- cash flow can be low after costs have been paid

- thorough research is needed to make the right decision and that can be costly

- investment strategy for your SMSF may need to be changed if it does not allow for buying property.

Business property

For many business owners, buying the building in which your business operates is one of the largest investment decisions they will ever make. Many people purchase the property in their own name and then want to transfer it into superannuation. This is allowed for business real property, but not residential property.

Business real property is defined as property used wholly and exclusively for business purposes. The business must also have an eligible interest in that property. While I have had many clients asking questions as to how to get around this definition from the ATO so they can transfer residential property into super, I can assure you the laws are very tight in this regard and you should not try to operate outside the law in any capacity.

Since the super laws changed, it has become possible to borrow money and purchase your business property inside your super fund. Given that a business owner controls the rent, and the property is owned by the super fund and can be sold free of capital gains tax at retirement, the benefits of owning business real property inside your fund are many.

Transferring business real property into your fund

If you want to transfer your business real property into your SMSF it is deemed a disposal for capital gains tax purposes and you will have to pay capital gains tax on the sale. Further, you will have to pay stamp duty at the rate of tax relevant to your state.

However, if you are eligible to use the small business capital gains tax rollover exemptions, you can reduce or eliminate your capital gains tax. I will describe this strategy in more detail in chapter 12, but there are four exemptions that can be used if your business assets are valued at less than $6 million:

¤ If you have owned the business for more than 15 years and are retiring (aged over 55 years) or permanently incapacitated, your asset will not be assessed for capital gains.

¤ As a small business owner, you will be eligible to receive a further 50 per cent capital gains discount (that is a further discount in addition to the 50 per cent discount for owning the asset for more than 12 months).

¤ You can roll over up to a lifetime $500 000 of capital gains (the funds have to go into super if you are aged less than 55).

¤ You can roll over the capital gain to be realised in a future year if you purchase a replacement asset.

For small business owners or commercial property investors, business real property can be a great way to increase your asset base. Business real property gives business owners greater control of their property investment and rent, which allows you some flexibility in the management of both the business and the property. Some of my clients have built significant wealth by investing in business real property when appropriate.

Derivatives

Like any investment inside your SMSF, you need to make sure you meet the obligations of the sole purpose test and ensure your investment strategy allows for investment in certain types of asset classes and with investment risk appropriate to members of the fund. Derivatives require a great deal of understanding and while they can increase gains, they can also magnify losses. These types of investments also require a great deal of education and I'd venture to say that they are simply inappropriate for 99.9 per cent of investors.

Derivatives are financial instruments, such as options, warrants and contracts for difference (CFDs), that give the investor leveraged exposure to movements in share or index price movements. Derivatives can be risky and investing in them may contravene the laws of SMSFs. Of particular interest is the structure of the financial instrument with a specific requirement to take the assets of the fund as collateral for a loan or margin call. If a CFD trade turns sour and more money is required in the trading account, this has been deemed different from the relationship of a margin lender with a margin call situation. So effectively no loan agreement has been entered into according to the ATO so a CFD is allowable under this notion. However, assets of the SMSF cannot be used as collateral in the trading account if the investor loses money and has to use collateral to repay the losses.

While derivatives should not even be a consideration for most investors, self-funding instalment warrants may be of interest to SMSFs. A self-funding instalment warrant is a financial product that allows an investor to borrow up to 70 per cent of the value of a share. An instalment warrant has a stop-loss attached to it, which means that if the share price falls below a particular level it will be automatically sold. The beauty of self-funding instalment warrants is that if you use them conservatively, borrowing 50 per cent or less of the cost, they may be cash-flow positive and a great way to borrow money inside your super fund and grow your share portfolio of blue-chip shares.

For example, if I bought $10 000 worth of a self-funding instalment warrant, borrowing 50 per cent of the cost, over a share in Commonwealth Bank (when it's valued at $50 a share) and it pays me a dividend of 6 per cent, then $5000 of that money would be lent to me. Let's say the borrowed funds ($5000) had a 9 per cent interest rate on them, then the cost of the loan would be $5000 × 9 per cent = $450 per year. If those $10 000 worth of CBA shares produced an income of 6 per cent in dividends then I would receive $600 of income per year, which is $150 more than the interest I have to pay on the loan. The difference can be used to reduce the capital owed.

Over time, as dividends rise (not always, but mostly), the cost of the interest paid may be dwarfed by the dividends, which will reduce the debt. You may also receive the franking credits in the SMSF, which will provide an additional benefit that can increase the size of your fund.

Over the right shares, self-funding instalment warrants can be a good investment, but they are not without risk. Self-funding instalment warrants provide the basis for the structure around purchasing property inside super funds as the principle is the same as is the structure required to purchase property by an SMSF.

With any investment in derivatives you need to exercise great care to ensure you do not contravene the investment rules for SMSFs, and to avoid magnifying your losses in the chase for better returns. Education and caution are the key to investing in derivatives, and abstinence will be appropriate for the majority.

Key points

¤ Cash and fixed interest are income investments that provide stability in volatile times.

¤ Shares and property can offer both income and capital growth, which helps your assets increase in value over time.

¤ SMSFs provide great flexibility for investing in direct assets, such as shares and property.

¤ You can borrow money to buy shares and property to magnify gains, but that can also mean magnifying losses.

¤ Carry out research before buying either shares or property, and avoid property spruikers.

¤ Caution and education are advised when considering investment in derivatives. See <www.asx.com.au>.

¤ Instalment warrants can be used to buy shares in an SMSF.

Portfolio management and asset allocation

Asset allocation—how you spread your money across different kinds of investments—is one of the most important aspects of managing your money in your self managed super fund. At its recent Australia-wide SMSF Roadshow, the ASX suggested that 98 per cent of your returns are a function of your asset allocation and just 2 per cent are the result of stock-picking. This means that your investment return will vary greatly depending on how much of your money is invested in each asset class—principally cash, fixed interest, shares or property.

We have seen regular 20 per cent rises and falls on global sharemarkets in recent years, so if your money was allocated 100 per cent to fixed interest, you would probably have had a better return on your money than if all your money had been invested in the sharemarket. However, depending on where in the sharemarket cycle you take your returns from, you may have been significantly better off holding shares for the long term. More than likely, you need a combination of asset classes to meet your needs and the requirements of the investment strategy of your SMSF.

As your exposure to riskier assets, such as shares and property, rises on the risk–return continuum (see figure 6.1, overleaf), so does the chance of loss or gain. Assessing your personal attitude towards risk is paramount in constructing a portfolio appropriate to the member/trustees of your

SMSF. So, too, your chosen asset allocation will need to match your written investment strategy in your SMSF.

Figure 6.1: risk and return

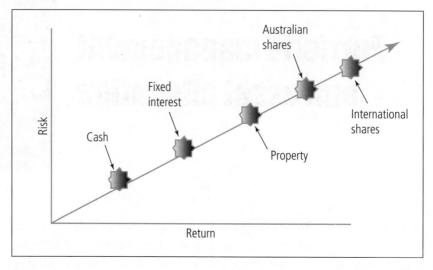

Your risk profile

As a sensible investor, you will need to decide on a long-term asset allocation that allows you to sleep at night—in other words, it suits your own attitude to risk—while providing the optimum long-term income and capital returns to suit your circumstances. Working out your attitude to risk is therefore an important first step in deciding on an asset allocation for your investments.

The Australian Securities and Investments Commission (ASIC) requires financial advisers to 'know their client', part of which requires advisers to undertake a risk profiling process with their clients. While risk profiling is a legal requirement, everyone interprets those requirements differently. At my company, Henderson Maxwell, we use a tool called FinaMetrica. We find that FinaMetrica gives us a quantitative solution in that it produces a number that represents your risk profile. The system augments that number by facilitating a client/adviser discussion around attitudes, experience and reaction to risk.

FinaMetrica asks a client 25 questions, and it then provides a suggested portfolio depending on their answers to the questions. We then have a long discussion around the client's experience in investing, current ownership of certain asset classes and their response to volatile economic times and risk management.

With FinaMetrica, the client signs off on feeling comfortable with the chosen asset allocation, which gives them more buy-in to the investment process. I encourage you to try the system in the abbreviated version given here, and if you have a partner who is not reading this book, I urge you to get them to do it, too. I guarantee that at least one of you will be surprised at the outcome and enjoy the process! The first seven questions are shown in the accompanying box. How would you and your partner answer them?

Risk profiling — the first seven questions from FinaMetrica

1 Compared with others, how do you rate your willingness to take financial risks?

You	Partner	(Select one)
☐	☐	Extremely low risk taker
☐	☐	Very low risk taker
☐	☐	Low risk taker
☐	☐	Average risk taker
☐	☐	High risk taker
☐	☐	Very high risk taker
☐	☐	Extremely high risk taker

2 How easily do you adapt when things go wrong financially?

You	Partner	(Select one)
☐	☐	Very uneasily
☐	☐	Somewhat uneasily
☐	☐	Somewhat easily
☐	☐	Very easily

(cont'd)

Risk profiling — the first seven questions from FinaMetrica *(cont'd)*

3 When you think of the word 'risk' in a financial context, which of the following words comes to mind first?

You	Partner	(Select one)
☐	☐	Danger
☐	☐	Uncertainty
☐	☐	Opportunity
☐	☐	Thrill

4 Have you ever invested a large sum in a risky investment mainly for the 'thrill' of seeing whether it went up or down in value?

You	Partner	(Select one)
☐	☐	No
☐	☐	Yes, but very rarely
☐	☐	Yes, somewhat rarely
☐	☐	Yes, somewhat frequently
☐	☐	Yes, very frequently

5 If you had to choose between more job security with a small pay increase and less job security with a big pay increase, which would you pick?

You	Partner	(Select one)
☐	☐	Definitely more job security with a small pay increase
☐	☐	Probably more job security with a small pay increase
☐	☐	Not sure
☐	☐	Probably less job security with a big pay increase
☐	☐	Definitely less job security with a big pay increase

6 When faced with a major financial decision, are you more concerned about the possible losses or the possible gains?

You	Partner	(Select one)
☐	☐	Always the possible losses
☐	☐	Usually the possible losses

☐	☐	Usually the possible gains
☐	☐	Always the possible gains

7 How do you usually feel about your major financial decisions after you make them?

Client Partner   (Select one)

☐	☐	Very pessimistic
☐	☐	Somewhat pessimistic
☐	☐	Somewhat optimistic
☐	☐	Very optimistic

Source: © FinaMetrica Pty Ltd.

What's your attitude towards risk?

And what are your fellow trustees' attitudes towards risk?

Each member of an SMSF may have a different response to certain market conditions and different attitudes to risk, which must be addressed in your fund's investment strategy. Importantly, the investments chosen must be appropriate to each member's investment objectives and income requirements. So, effectively, you may need to have different investments for different members.

More often than not, couples find a happy medium and invest appropriately, but conflicts may arise. For example, if adult children are members of the fund when Mum and Dad are drawing an account-based pension income, the adult children will be looking for capital growth with a longer time frame than Mum and Dad, who will be needing more income and less volatility in the sharemarket. Be aware that different strategies may be required to satisfy the investment objectives of different members, which may even be a reason to leave the kids out of your SMSF altogether, as different strategies may necessitate paying higher fees through brokerage, having to create a more complex investment strategy and for the annual administration of the fund by your accountant.

> **Tip**
>
> You can use FinaMetrica by following the link on my website <www.samhenderson.com.au>. For just $55 you can undertake the full FinaMetrica risk profile questionnaire process and receive your result, or you can just download the questionnaire for free, also at my site. I would suggest going through the whole process to ascertain your risk profile, as it truly reflects your attitude towards risk management, which will help you make better investment decisions. I'd also suggest you have a discussion about risk and sign off on your risk profile ensuring to include other member trustees, if in fact you have additional members in your fund.

Most industry or retail super funds simply put members into an investment option with a balanced risk profile as the default option when you don't make an active investment choice, which most funds now allow you to do. But what does 'balanced' actually mean? The answer is that it can mean completely different things, depending on which company you are invested with. Balanced may mean that you have 50 per cent of your super account invested in shares and 50 per cent invested in cash and fixed interest, but it can also mean that you have up to 75 per cent invested in shares and 25 per cent invested in cash and fixed interest. In volatile markets, this variation can have a marked difference on the investment return on your life savings. In rising markets, it may also mean that you miss out on good returns if you have too much money invested in cash and fixed interest.

The other thing that happens out there in superannuation land is that different products have different names, so what one fund calls balanced, another might call balanced conservative or balanced growth or any number of similar things. How the average punter interprets this terminology is beyond me and it's no wonder most people have inappropriate investment allocations and are not interested in their superannuation.

Table 6.1 shows what's typically meant by each of the industry terms for different kinds of asset allocation.

Table 6.1: typical asset allocation terms used by commercial super funds

Investment choice	Cash/Fixed interest %	Shares %
Cash or Stable	100	0
Conservative	25–50	50–75
Balanced	30–50	50–70
Growth	10–30	70–90
High growth	0–15	85–100

Shares can mean Australian shares, international shares, property securities or even alternative investments, such as infrastructure projects or exchange-traded funds (ETFs); and cash/fixed interest can mean actual liquid cash, term deposits, government bonds, corporate bonds or even mortgage-backed securities. All of these alternatives have different risk profiles and behave in different ways depending on market conditions. To confuse the matter even further, the products will differ from provider to provider, which is why many SMSF members simply choose to invest into assets that they can access and understand, such as term deposits, Australian shares, and direct residential or commercial property. The ATO website confirms this in their asset allocation tables, which indicate the simplicity of the asset allocation for SMSFs.

If you don't understand where your money is or how it's invested, then you probably shouldn't have it in that investment. I changed my business model many years ago to eliminate managed funds and structured products because neither my clients nor I had much insight into how those funds were invested, and they simply weren't liquid enough. That means that you can't sell them when you want to, and in fact many mortgage-backed funds are still frozen many years after the GFC hit. Managed funds take around two weeks to sell down and the unit price may be struck over a week of trading. In the past few years, a week can mean a 10 per cent differential in pricing.

If you own direct shares, you can sell them immediately into the market and have your money in three days after settlement. The point is that we can target a price at which to sell or choose to sell at market at more or less a precise point in time.

The other key issue many investors face is that most cash accounts or cash options within retail and industry super funds pay miserly returns, when online accounts, available to SMSFs, offer interest rates 1 to 2 per cent better than a regular super fund does. Moreover, many super funds don't even offer term deposits as an option to increase cash returns for investors. These are all reasons for choosing SMSFs over regular super funds.

Risk management

As a financial adviser, my job is all about risk management and I often say to people that risk management is about avoiding bad investments as much as finding great investments. Think of those friends and family who have gone chasing high returns and lost their money, or had their money tied up in illiquid funds, trusts or investments. Making a mistake by choosing the wrong type of investment or having too much exposure to a certain asset can have devastating effects on your life savings and can be very expensive.

Risk management is therefore the process of assessing each investment and understanding both its positives and negatives. How much can you afford to lose if share or property markets fall 10 per cent, 20 per cent or even 50 per cent? How will you fund your retirement if such an event occurs? These questions are not asked enough by investors, as risk management research indicates that investors take a very optimistic view of a new investment and don't think much about the risk of loss.

An essential part of successful investing is constructing an investment process that matches the investment strategy for your SMSF. For example, in my business we follow a five-step investment process before we invest a cent. It looks like this:

◻ *Economic research* — this addresses the growth of a country's gross domestic product (GDP), manufacturing output, unemployment levels and interest rates. These leading economic indicators are your barometer for the future health of our economy and will help you navigate sharemarkets. For example, countries with high unemployment may have low GDP growth and low consumption and may not be a good place to invest.

◻ *Sector analysis* — within the chosen country or region, which sectors of the economy will benefit from the prevailing economic and business trends. For example, in Australia, the resources sector has been strong and manufacturing has been weak so you may be better served investing in resources shares than in retail shares. For example, buy BHP and sell David Jones.

¤   *Company analysis*—we try to identify companies that may benefit from prevailing economic and business conditions, or even companies that might suffer, so we can eliminate them from selection for our potential portfolio. Survival of the fittest or the natural selection process may be terms used to describe this method.

¤   *Company valuations*—we look for companies that represent good value and identify which are currently overpriced. We then work out a price we are willing to pay for certain companies, so we can take advantage of opportunities when they arise.

¤   *The transaction*—once we have identified a company as being worthy of purchase, we then work out what price we want to pay for it. In calculating how much of the stock to buy, we may also consider its overall weighting on the sharemarket; for example, BHP makes up around 12 per cent of the total value of all shares listed on the ASX so we may aim to hold around 12 per cent or even more if we really like the company.

This five-step process allows us to navigate choppy waters without emotion and without reacting to media articles of boom and doom. We have our own investment selection process that operates independently of the fear and greed being sold to you in the newspapers, and on radio and television. More often than not, when sharemarkets decrease significantly, opportunities abound, but that's when everyone is selling—and that's when I am buying. As investment guru Warren Buffett says, 'Be greedy when others are fearful and fearful when others are greedy'.

Tip

Having your own investment research and decision-making process in place means you can take the emotion out of investing and rely on the system to do its job. The five-step process works for me.

You need to develop your own process and understanding of when and how you will implement your investment strategy for your SMSF. Since the GFC, the world has become a different place and investing takes on new meaning when sharemarkets can move 5 per cent in a day or 50 per cent in a year. Not only do you need a thorough understanding of the sharemarket but you also need to be well versed in property, fixed interest and cash, and in all the rules and regulations that accompany Australia's complex superannuation laws.

> **Tip**
>
> Ninety-eight per cent of your returns will come from asset allocation and not stock-picking, so don't get too carried away with trying to pick the next BHP.

Asset allocation

In my first book, *Financial Planning DIY Guide*, which explains each asset class and how to access them for the best results, I wrote about the importance of asset allocation and how it will affect your final investment returns from both an income and a capital perspective. Asset allocation is one of the most important aspects of managing your SMSF appropriately.

In my own business, we spend more time on asset allocation than stock-picking because asset allocation is the biggest driver of investment return. You need to understand this before getting stuck into researching which shares you will buy from your newly cashed-up superannuation fund. Don't be in a hurry, take your time to find the asset mix that will suit you and keep in mind that the investment environment is everchanging. Today's prevailing mood can change in an instant, and you want to be ready for change, whether that change is big or small, or up or down in sharemarkets or property markets.

> **Tip**
>
> Asset allocation is the single most important factor in developing your investment strategy so that it will match the risk profiles of members and set expectations for investment returns.

Eat well sleep well theory

In considering the right mix of assets in your total investment portfolio, you need to be able to pass the sleep test. The eat well sleep well theory goes something like this; while you may eat well when share and property markets are rising, you may not sleep well when they start falling.

There's a lot to be said for security. I can guarantee that markets will change and fluctuate over time. In fact, it's a sure thing and you need to be prepared for either situation—a rising market or a falling market. If your asset allocation is right, you will not panic if either occurs, and then you won't be forced to sell when prices are low or to buy when prices are high.

Everyone wants the same thing

I remember one of my first mentors in the financial planning industry said to me one day, 'Everyone wants the same thing, Sam. They want to see their assets go up in value and they want those assets to produce an income, particularly when they retire. They want their investments to be secure because they hate losing money, and they don't want to pay tax if they don't have to. Everyone basically wants the same thing'.

He was absolutely right and I have been testing his theory for more than a decade with success—everyone does actually want the same thing. What varies is that some people have higher expectations for returns, where others are quite happy with a moderate return over the long term. As Buffett put it, some people are greedy and other people are fearful. Importantly, each investment portfolio needs to be tailored to the individual members in the SMSF to ensure the investment strategy is appropriate to every individual in the fund. Those individuals should then acknowledge their comfort by signing the investment strategy as a matter of best practice.

Growth versus income

While capital growth may be a key reason to own an asset, the other main reason is income, which comes in the form of interest, dividends or rent depending on the nature of the investment. If you invest into cash, you are investing only for income as there is no growth in cash investments. It can barely be described as an investment for this reason as there is zero chance of capital growth. However, your money is relatively safe in cash and if that makes you comfortable then it is an appropriate place to park your money.

If you invest into shares they will have dividends, which is the term for how companies distribute a portion of their profits to their shareholders. For example, different companies have different policies for distributing their profits (earnings) to shareholders. All companies, listed on the ASX or otherwise, have a key objective of making a profit, but that's where things start to differ. Some companies like to distribute all their profits back to investors, and others will distribute a smaller amount or none at all.

As an SMSF trustee and the creator and manager of the written investment strategy, you will need to choose the types of investments most suitable to meet the objectives of members (see figure 6.2). You will need to decide whether growth or income is most important and that may be determined by members' ages, life stages, income requirements for pensions, attitudes towards risk, previous investment experience and a host of other factors that will need to be considered when investing for your SMSF.

Figure 6.2: when it comes to investment, everyone wants the same four things

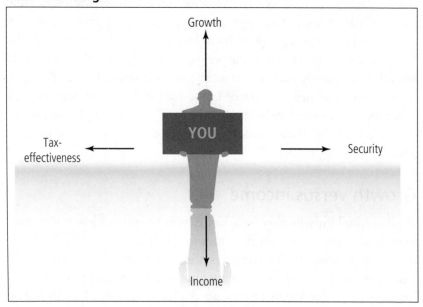

Key points

¤ Risk management is fundamental to your chosen investment direction.

¤ Ensure your written investment strategy is appropriate and updated regularly.

¤ You need to understand the attitude to risk of all members of the fund and consider that in formulating the SMSF's investment strategy.

¤ The lion's share of investment return will be a function of asset allocation and not stock-picking.

¤ When it comes to investment, everyone wants growth, income, security and tax-effectiveness.

CHAPTER 7

Borrowing in super to buy shares or property

Borrowing and spending is not the way to prosperity.
Paul Ryan, US politician

If you want to borrow money inside your SMSF you need to understand the key rules of SMSFs, including the sole purpose test and the fact that you are generally not permitted to borrow money inside your super fund—except under limited circumstances and provided you have a particular structure for borrowing in place, called a warrant or a limited recourse loan. You cannot risk the other assets held by your super fund by using them as collateral for a loan. Trustees have an obligation to invest fund money in a way that protects the future payment of retirement benefits to members and to protect the members' capital by employing prudent investment strategies, as detailed in the written investment strategy.

From 24 September 2007, section 67 of the *Superannuation Industry (Supervision) Act 1993* (SIS Act) has allowed for borrowing inside super, but only under a limited recourse borrowing arrangement (also known as a warrant, debt instalment trust, or bare trust) to acquire a single acquirable asset (shares in a single company, one piece of real estate property, and to maintain and repair the asset. Further clarification was given on 7 July 2010 to clear up some points.

The July 2010 clarification includes the statement that trustees cannot use borrowed funds to improve the asset, for example by carrying out renovations or development of properties; it also provides further protection for trustees from default. Also clarified was the fact that the loan structure is only applicable to a single asset or multiple units of a single type of investment, such as shares in one company. If you want multiple assets, then you need a separate trust to hold each individual asset — that is, a limited recourse loan structure (warrant) for each asset. For example, each property will need a different structure, and so will different shares or a portfolio of shares, although you can purchase multiple units of the same asset at the same price, for example a portfolio of BHP shares. This means that you cannot buy a portfolio of different shares and borrow against it; however, you could borrow against holdings in a managed fund or exchange traded fund that contained a group of different assets, such as a diversified share portfolio. It also means that multiple structures would be required for each property if you were looking to buy multiple properties.

If you are interested in investigating the benefits of borrowing in super, you must ensure your trust deed allows for borrowing and that your investment strategy details a method by which you can borrow, which encompasses your overall investment objectives. In a practical sense, this may mean updating your trust deed (cost around $500 to $1000) and rewriting your investment strategy (about two to three hours' work or seek assistance from your adviser).

Borrowing in super can be a little complex and expensive, but from my experience the benefits far outweigh the costs for the right people who have the right risk profile (higher risk and longer time frame), income (high income) and super contributions (ability to maximise super contributions). I strongly recommend you seek advice from your adviser or administrator on how to structure your fund to borrow, or see my website at <www.samhenderson.com.au>, because the law is very strict and constantly changing.

A final word of warning: while borrowing can magnify your profits, it can also magnify your losses by significantly increasing risk and there is nothing worse than owing more than you own, while having to go on repaying a loan on a poor investment that you cannot sell. This is the worst kind of liability, so try not to go into an investment with too much optimism, always understand your risks and cash flows, and make sure you have an exit strategy in place before you make an investment to ensure you can minimise your losses.

If you are interested in borrowing (also called gearing) in your fund, perhaps start with a smaller amount and work your way up, and remember that all markets can fall in value. Property prices are not guaranteed to keep rising and share prices can be volatile. Caveat emptor—let the buyer beware—definitely applies here!

How borrowing works in super

Borrowing in superannuation is only permitted if you use an instalment warrant structure to buy either shares or property. Essentially, without this structure in place borrowing inside of superannuation is not permitted.

An instalment warrant is a structure that allows an investor to borrow money by making a cash part-payment on an asset and taking out a loan on the balance. An instalment warrant is a limited recourse loan, which is essential in the context of an SMSF, because the lender can repossess only the asset for which the loan is secured in the event of default (non-payment of the loan). The other assets in the SMSF will remain unencumbered and therefore secure to meet your retirement needs.

The balance of the loan is repaid in instalments. Instalment warrants have been a popular way to buy shares as you can put down a deposit of, say, 50 per cent of the value of the shares and borrow the balance over a number of years, often five years, and use the dividends earned to repay the debt over that time. While the instalment warrant is in place and you are repaying the debt, the actual shares are held by a custodian, such as RBS or Westpac. At the end of the five-year period, the debt is paid and the asset becomes yours (the beneficial owner) or your SMSF's. You pay no capital gains tax or stamp duty when the shares are transferred from the custodian to you.

The company that lends you the money to buy the instalment warrants only holds the shares as collateral, or security, for that loan. If the shares fall below a certain value, the company lending the money will have a stop-loss in place to limit their potential loan loss. A stop-loss is an automatic sales order on the shares that ensures they are sold if their price falls below a certain value. If this occurs, you can lose your investment entirely, hence the inherent risk in this kind of borrowing, and the objective of not gearing too highly, for example borrowing no more than 50 per cent of the value of the asset. If the value of the shares falls to the stop-loss level, your shares will be sold and you will lose the cash that you used for the deposit, as well as any equity built up since your purchase of the shares.

Instalment warrants are based on what is called a limited recourse loan. It is limited to the asset for which the intended investment was made. The company giving you the loan cannot make a claim over your house, car or other superannuation assets in the event of default but they will sell your shares under the agreement that they make with you—described in the product disclosure statement (PDS).

For risk management purposes, most institutions won't lend more than 70 per cent of the value of an asset to decrease their risk. I recommend that you do not borrow more than 50 per cent if you don't have a lot of experience with warrant structures and limited recourse loans.

If you buy a property in your super fund, the bank will not have a stop-loss in place in the event of default, but they will ask you to kick in more money or they will repossess the property. Often the bank will also ask for a personal guarantee or they will take security over your house or other non-super assets to protect their financial risk. So despite an instalment warrant structure and perhaps the existence of a limited recourse loan for the purpose of meeting the SMSF requirements, the bank may well ask for further collateral and security over your personal assets, and who can blame them? Limited recourse loans brought the United States to its knees during the GFC, and conservative Australian banks, which own 96 per cent of the property loans market, will hardly allow you to simply walk away from a dud investment.

When you buy share-based instalment warrants from providers such as RBS (Royal Bank of Scotland), Macquarie or Westpac, their legal teams have constructed the terms and conditions under which they are willing to operate. You simply sign the paperwork as an investor and operate under their terms and the suppliers are not willing to negotiate.

These share-based instalment warrants are called self-funding instalment warrants because the dividends from the shares are used to repay the loan over time.

Tip

Go to the ASX website at <www.asx.com.au> and download its booklets on self-funding instalment warrants so you have a detailed source of information on how these warrants operate. Some worked examples are included.

If you are buying property through a limited recourse loan facility in super, many lenders (such as the major banks) are developing their own contracts and framework, but the industry is still young, which is why the legal costs can be up to $3000, depending on which lender you choose. Lawyers are also developing loan contracts and they do vary to the point where banks are recommending certain legal firms because they are familiar with their documentation. As you can imagine, the paperwork required to establish an agreement with a lender who is willing to provide you with a limited recourse loan is detailed but not overly arduous. With properties, things are a little more complicated than buying an instalment warrant over shares, where the details are set out in a product disclosure statement (PDS) and you simply sign off on the issuer's agreement. Don't let a little paperwork put you off investing in property through your super fund.

Tip

Try to avoid property spruikers, who make up to 5 per cent commission on the sale of new properties from property developers, and additional commissions from finance companies. Also avoid properties that need rental guarantees to sell them because the rent or the tenants may dry up after the guarantee period.

Self-funding instalment warrants to purchase shares

Self-funding instalment warrants allow you to borrow money over shares listed on the ASX. Providers of instalment warrant products will provide a list of shares for which they are willing to lend you money, and the maximum percentage of borrowing that they are willing to lend. For example, they may be willing to lend up 75 per cent of the value on Commonwealth Bank Share warrants but only 50 per cent of the value of Oz Minerals warrants.

Let's look at an example (see table 7.1). Let's say I have $200000 in my super fund that I am willing to gear into Commonwealth Bank shares, assuming the share price is $50 per share. With a 50 per cent loan to value ratio (50 per cent LVR)—which means I will borrow 50 per cent of the value of the shares—I could borrow an additional $200000 and buy $400000 worth of CBA shares. I would have a loan with an effective interest rate of 9 per cent ($18000 per year) and dividends starting at $24000 per year, assuming a 6 per cent dividend rate, and excluding franking credits (your franking credits are credited to your SMSF, but not your loan account so they can't be used to reduce debt, though they will increase the balance of your SMSF).

Over a 10-year period, the shares would pay themselves off (hence the term self-funding instalment warrant), and assuming an annual growth rate of 5 per cent on the share price, your equity could triple over the period. If you used your tax-effective super contributions and franking credits to reduce the debt, you would be able to pay your debt off within three to five years, or you could use the cash flow from the dividends to fund other purchases to help you diversify your investments (see table 7.1 to see how your investment would work).

Keep in mind that share prices rarely increase in a simple linear fashion and certain shares will perform better than others. Different shares will also produce different levels of dividends, but the higher the dividend, the faster you will be able to repay your debt. This strategy is not without risk and caution must be used whenever you borrow someone else's money.

That being said, for higher income earners and those capable of making regular maximum contributions to super, this strategy can work well to accumulate assets in a highly tax-effective manner and repay debt faster, which reduces risk fairly quickly. I suggest borrowing a maximum of 50 per cent of the value of the shares, though this can be increased depending on your circumstances and attitude to risk, but my advice is to keep it conservative if you have any doubt.

Table 7.1: summary of how using instalment warrants to buy shares can work

Year	Share price	Portfolio value	Interest	Dividend	Debt	Equity
0	$50	$400 000	$18 000	$24 000	$200 000	$200 000
1	$53	$420 000	$17 460	$25 200	$194 000	$226 000
2	$55	$441 000	$16 763	$26 460	$186 260	$254 740
3	$58	$463 050	$15 891	$27 783	$176 563	$286 487
4	$61	$486 203	$14 820	$29 172	$164 671	$321 531
5	$64	$510 513	$13 529	$30 631	$150 319	$360 193
6	$67	$536 038	$11 990	$32 162	$133 217	$402 821
7	$70	$562 840	$10 174	$33 770	$113 045	$449 796
8	$74	$590 982	$8 050	$35 459	$89 448	$501 534
9	$78	$620 531	$5 584	$37 232	$62 040	$558 492
10	$81	$651 558	$2 735	$39 093	$30 391	$621 167

Note: Calculations assume 9 per cent interest on loan; 6 per cent dividend per year; and 5 per cent growth per year in value of shares, with all dividends used to repay the debt (excluding franking credits).

Using instalment warrants to purchase property

The paperwork for buying a property via a property warrant is more complex, and even though some standard templated documents are available, banks have their legal teams sift through the details to ensure they are comfortable with the legal structure. In some cases they will provide a list of approved property warrant structures or providers (legal firms) that they are willing to accept. Figure 7.1 (overleaf) gives you an idea of how a property warrant is structured for the purchase of a single property.

Remember, you only need this structure if you are planning to use borrowed money in your SMSF. If you are paying cash for a property, you do not need to use a property warrant at all and you will not need these structures in place. These structures are designed to protect the assets of the SMSF from lenders and maintain the sole purpose test of ensuring that you have money to fund your retirement.

Figure 7.1: how an instalment warrant can be structured to purchase property

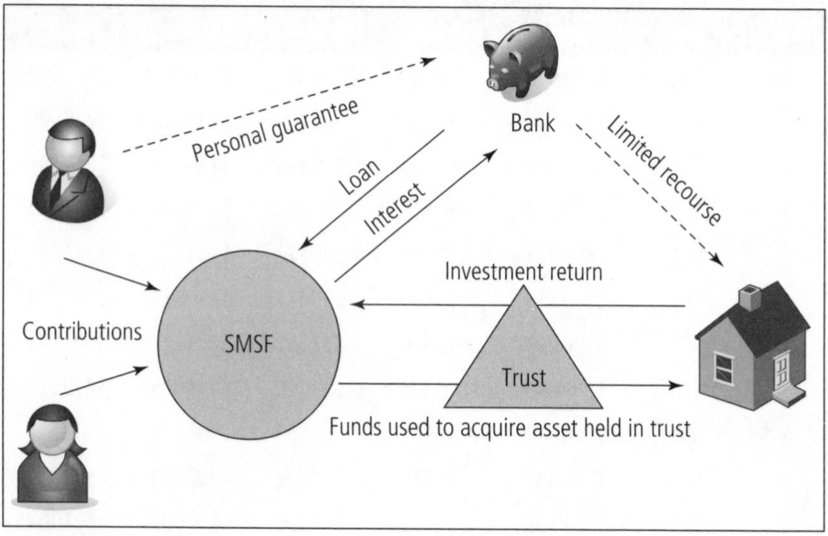

Source: © BT Financial Group 2011.

Let me walk you through figure 7.1 step by step. This is how a property warrant works. I'll use the terms a bank would use to keep the language consistent for when you start communicating with the bank, but keep in mind that most bank lenders won't know how to deal with SMSFs, so speak to a specialist.

¤   First, to borrow through your SMSF, you need an SMSF that has a corporate trustee, which may cost you another $600 to $1000 to establish if you don't already have one in place. You may also need an update of your existing trust deed to ensure it allows for a limited recourse loan. You will also need to update your written investment strategy if necessary to allow for the purchase of the property and provision of the cash deposit. Do not attempt this without professional and experienced advice.

- Your SMSF is represented by the large round circle with the trustees, who make regular super contributions to the fund from superannuation (concessional or non-concessional) on the left. That's you and your fellow member/trustees.

- The new asset (it has to be a new asset) that you are planning to purchase will need to be held by a custodian, in other words, another trust structure with another corporate trustee that is separate from your main SMSF and its corporate trustee. This second corporate trustee is the name in which the property and the loan will be held. For example Henderson Property No. 2 Pty Ltd. This is known by the banks as the custodian: it is a structure under which the limited recourse loan must operate. When the debt has been extinguished, the asset will pass to the SMSF free of capital gains tax and stamp duty. The purpose of the second trust is to segregate the asset and to ensure that the lender has recourse only against the asset held by the custodian.

- The new property that you are acquiring will be purchased in the name of the custodian and transferred to the name of the super fund only after the debt is paid off.

- The bank will lend the money to the custodian and your superannuation contributions and rent can be used to reduce the property debt over time. Most banks will lend a maximum of 72 per cent of the value of the property, so you need a deposit of at least 28 per cent of the value of the property plus stamp duty and other costs. You need to ensure that the debt level matches the risk profile and investment strategy of members, so perhaps a lower debt ratio may be appropriate but many properties are cash-flow positive when you have a 30 per cent deposit.

- The bank may require personal guarantees for the debt as further collateral, but try to resist this if you can to reduce your own risk and leave the bank to carry as much risk as possible. You may have to make a larger deposit to justify this.

Banks generally handle SMSF borrowing quite poorly, because of the complexity of the structures involved and a lack of education that would ensure they understood how it all works. After all, it is a very specialist area. My advice is to contact an SMSF expert who has actually completed a number of these transactions (don't use a first-timer!) and avoid local banks or property spruikers, as they will not give you the full picture (and may waste your time) and you risk non-compliance.

> **Tip**
>
> For more information contact me at <www.samhenderson.com.au> or visit the ATO website at <www.ato.gov.au> and type in 'limited recourse borrowing' and a host of information will pop up.

Conditions of borrowing money in your SMSF

The following conditions for borrowing through an SMSF to purchase property were updated and clarified on 7 July 2010. These now state:

⌶ You can borrow money only to buy a single asset or a group of identical assets—for example; a single property or a group of shares in the same company at the same price that can be treated as a single asset or acquirable asset, under the legislation.

⌶ You cannot use borrowed money to improve or develop a property.

⌶ You may not substantially change the nature of the property— for example, subdivide or develop a property, which may include rezoning or multidevelopment.

⌶ The asset must be held by the custodian of the second trust, and the trustees have a beneficial right to ownership of that asset (the bank has the mortgage) and may purchase the asset with one or more payments at any time. For example, the asset is in the name of Henderson Property No. 2 Pty Ltd, and the bank holds the mortgage until the property is paid off, when it is transferred into the name of your SMSF or your SMSF's main corporate trustee.

¤ No other lender can apply a charge (no second mortgages) to the asset, apart from the original lender who holds the security over the asset.

¤ The acquirable asset can be replaced by another acquirable asset in limited circumstances (stipulated under Section 67 of the SIS Act).

One outcome of these new rules is that you need a new custodian and trust for each asset so if you want to buy multiple properties then you need multiple trusts. That means you need a corporate trustee (custodian) and a new bare trust for each new asset or property. It may be possible to use the same corporate trustee, so that each property is in the same name, given that the property is purchased in the name of the corporate trustee and is transferred into the name of the SMSF when the debt is repaid.

When investing in share-based warrants, the lenders or product suppliers provide all the documentation and structures, so you don't have to worry about it. At the time of writing, Commonwealth Bank of Australia were offering an all-in-one product to cover property purchases, but the costs were significantly higher when compared with the approach outlined above. It may make things easier, but by my calculations it would cost around $50000 more over a five-year period for the purchase of a $500000 property, when taking into account a higher interest rate, application fees, monthly account fees and establishment costs. It's best to shop around or, better still, seek advice until these structures become more mainstream.

Another issue that has arisen out of these changes is that you cannot use borrowed money to make improvements to the properties or to develop properties. You must use capital that is already in the fund to do this. You need to be careful not to be seen by the ATO as carrying on a business of property development, as this may constitute non-compliance because of the sole purpose test for all super funds. To say that borrowing inside of super is a whole new ball game is an understatement and caution is required at each step.

Figure 7.2 (overleaf) shows the steps required to set up an SMSF and purchase a property with borrowed money.

Figure 7.2: setting up an SMSF to borrow money to buy property

Choose a name and decide members

Choose a name for your SMSF. Decide who will be the members and the trustees of the fund (up to four people).

Trust deeds and corporate trustee

Seek professional help from a financial adviser/accountant/solicitor to prepare the trust deeds that create your SMSF. If you are intending to purchase an investment property in your SMSF, you will need to create a company that will act as trustee of the SMSF. The members will be directors of that company. You will need a second corporate trustee and trust established that will sit inside the main structure of your SMSF. This corporate trustee is to be the purchaser of the property. Once debt is repaid, this structure can be closed and the asset will pass to the main SMSF.

ATO registration

Register your SMSF with the ATO.

(This is something that your professional adviser should do as part of their service).

Open bank account

Open a bank account in the name of the SMSF and rollover your super accounts from other funds to consolidate your superannuation, ready to invest. Remember to give these bank details to your work so that they can deposit future SG contributions into your SMSF from now on.

Write an investment strategy

The trustees of the SMSF must write an investment strategy. This is required by superannuation law. If you are intending to purchase an investment property inside your SMSF your strategy must reflect this. It must also reflect the risk profile of members, treatment of cash for pensions and diversification.

Implement investment strategy

Now you can commence investing your superannuation monies according to your investment strategy. You will need to:

- obtain finance FIRST so you know how much you can borrow and repay
- prepare deposit money to be made available
- start looking for appropriately priced property (don't look for property first)
- exchange contract once property is found in name of second corporate trustee (custodian)
- property settlement and finalisation
- property management and review.

Regularly review your SMSF and investment strategy

Your SMSF should be reviewed at least once every six months.
Items to review include cash flows, asset performance, members' contributions, adherence to the investment strategy, tax obligations, minimum pension payments, and so on.

Buying property in your SMSF versus in your own name

One of the dilemmas that will arise with buying property is what entity to purchase the property in. Should you put it in your own name or the SMSF's? In table 7.2, the various tax rates are illustrated for personally owned assets versus those in the super fund.

Table 7.2: tax rates on personal versus super fund assets*

How much tax could you be paying on your personal investments?	How much tax could you be paying on your superannuation investments?
¤ Up to 46.5% if your total income is over $180 000	¤ 15% if the assets are held in your SMSF and you are still working.
¤ Up to 38.5% if your total income is under $180 000	¤ 0% of your assets are held in your SMSF and you are drawing a pension.
¤ Up to 31.5% if your total income is under $80 000	
¤ Up to 16.5% if your total income is under $37 000	
¤ 0% if your income is less than $6000 per annum	

Note: Capital gains tax is payable at your normal marginal rate of income tax for the year in which the contract is exchanged for the sale of a property. Capital gains tax is 0% if a property is sold when you are retired or 10% if you have owned it for more than 12 months inside super.

* Based on 2011–12 financial year tax rates.

Table 7.3 (overleaf) illustrates some of the advantages of owning an investment property in your SMSF or individually.

Table 7.3: comparison of owning property in an SMSF versus personal ownership

Comparison point	SMSF	Individual
Tax on rent	Taxed at 15% while members are working. **Taxed at 0% once members are retired and drawing a pension.**	Taxed at marginal tax rate (up to 46.5%) regardless of whether members are working or have retired.
Capital gains tax	Taxed at 15% if asset owned for less than 12 months. Taxed at 10% if asset owned for more than 12 months. **No capital gains tax payable if members are retired and drawing a pension.**	Taxed at marginal tax rate (up to 46.5%) regardless of whether members are working or are retired.
Access to rent as a form of income	Can only be withdrawn from the SMSF as a pension over age 55.	Can be accessed at any time.
Use of the investment property	Cannot be used for personal use by the members of the fund or any person related to the members of the fund.	Can be accessed for personal use at any time.
Deposit required	30–40%	5–20%
Cash flow	Loan repayments are made from a combination of rent, personal contributions, deductible contributions and your employer contributions.	Loan repayments are made from rent and your surplus income.
Tax-effective loan repayments	By making a concessional contribution to your SMSF and using that cash to repay the loan, you will have more money available after tax to make repayments. Thus, your loan will be paid off sooner.	All repayments on the loan are made with after-tax dollars. Your personal tax rate may be as high as 46.5%. After tax that leaves 53.5 cents to make any additional loan repayments.

Note: For example, concessional contributions are taxed at 15%. Any concessional contributions are then deducted from your gross salary, further reducing your tax liability. For every dollar you contribute to superannuation you will have 85 cents left after tax to make additional loan repayments.

What type of property can a self managed superannuation fund own?

An SMSF allows its members the freedom to control where their superannuation money is invested. However, there are rules around what type of property an SMSF can own. The following Q&A will help answer some of your questions.

Can my SMSF own a residential investment property?

Yes, but within certain conditions. A member cannot transfer an existing residential investment property that they own in their own name into their SMSF. However, an SMSF can buy a residential investment property from a person or entity who has no connection with the SMSF. To meet the sole purpose test, any residential investment properties must be leased or rented on an arm's length basis to a third party who is not family or a business relation of any of the members of the SMSF. This prohibits spouses, children, siblings, parents, grandparents, nephews and nieces, in-laws and mistresses from occupying the property that is owned by the SMSF.

Can my SMSF own my business premises?

Yes. If a member of an SMSF operates a business that owns the premises in which it operates, that real business property can be transferred into the SMSF or purchased by the SMSF. The business is then required under superannuation legislation to pay normal market rent to the SMSF for the use of that real business property. Be aware that, if you are transferring the property into the SMSF, there are limits on the value of assets that can be transferred into an SMSF. Current legislation allows for each member to transfer up to $450 000 as a non-concessional contribution into your SMSF. For example, if your business has two shareholders (for example, Mum and Dad), then a property to the total value of $900 000 can be transferred into the SMSF during a three-year period.

Can my SMSF own my principal place of residence (the family home)?

No. A member's principal residence cannot be owned by an SMSF. Superannuation legislation strictly prohibits an SMSF owning the family home. This would contravene the sole purpose test, as a member or members would be gaining a benefit from an asset owned by the SMSF, whose sole purpose is to provide a retirement benefit. Living rent-free or paying below market rent for a home to live in may seem like a nice benefit, but it is not allowed.

Can my SMSF own my holiday home?

No. A holiday home cannot be owned by an SMSF. This contravenes the sole purpose test. Even if you intend to hire out the holiday home for any amount of time and intend to use it only for you and your family for one or two weeks a year, it will still contravene the sole purpose test and is not permitted by superannuation legislation. The members or any relatives of a member of the SMSF cannot use the property for personal use.

Interestingly, under current legislation, you could borrow money to buy a property in your SMSF, pay it off with tax-effective super contributions and rent, and then at retirement (after age 60, when it will be tax-free to do so) cash it out of the SMSF and live in it.

Can I transfer my investment property to my SMSF?

No. Residential investment properties cannot be transferred to an SMSF under the current superannuation laws. You can buy a new residential property inside your SMSF but not transfer existing residential properties. Commercial property and business properties can be transferred to SMSFs from personal names.

Case study: using borrowed money to buy a property in your SMSF

James and Cindy are both 50 years old and have recently established an SMSF with a $400 000 balance that has been rolled over from a pooled superannuation industry fund ($300 000 from James and $100 000 from Cindy). James earns $150 000 a year and Cindy is on $60 000 a year. James is contributing $50 000 to super and Cindy is comfortable putting $25 000 into super each year through salary sacrifice.

James and Cindy establish the correct structures to allow them to purchase a property inside their SMSF, including updating their trust deed, adding a corporate trustee and, for the sake of borrowing money to buy the property, an additional corporate trustee (custodian) with a bare trust to hold the property until the debt is repaid. Total set-up cost was around $3000 for the documentation, plus another $2000 for advice. Remember, if they can afford to buy the property outright, they do not need this structure at all.

They have found a two-bedroom unit in Sydney's inner west, costing $500 000, and put down a deposit of $200 000 and borrow $300 000. The property is rented at $500 per week, or $26 000 a year. Allowing for annual expenses of $2500, their net income is $23 500 a year. Bank interest is charged at a rate of 9 per cent—a little higher than a regular home loan—resulting in an interest payment of $27 000 a year. In the first year the property is potentially cash-flow negative by $3500.

However, if James and Cindy put their super contributions and excess income towards their debt reduction strategy, their debt will fall from $300 000 to $234 012 after the first year of ownership because the contributions and positive cash flow will help reduce their debt. Their super contributions of $75 000 (combined), less 15 per cent contributions tax, will reduce their debt by at least $63 750 in year one, when combined with their positive cash flow from the rent.

Their net rental income (rent minus strata fees) remains at $23 500 assuming rent remains stable, but their interest bill has dropped in line with their debt level to $21 061, which would make them cash-flow positive by the end of year one. They will continue to use their tax-effective super contributions to reduce their debt further by the end of year two by another $63 750 ($75 000 less 15 per cent super contributions tax) to just $159 486 when combined with the positive cash flow from the rent.

(cont'd)

Case study: using borrowed money to buy a property in your SMSF *(cont'd)*

In year three James and Cindy continue to repay their debt with their tax-effective super contributions and their cash-flow positive income stream from the property rent. Interest is now only $14353 a year, and they have raised the rent by $25 per week, so income has also increased. Expenses remained steady at $2500 per annum, which includes a maintenance allowance, agent's fees and strata fees. So in year three their property is producing positive cash flow of $9430 and they are still contributing their $63750 (after contributions tax) to their fund, which is used to reduce their debt to just $80852.

In addition, the property has risen in value by 5 per cent a year and it is now worth $578813, with just $80852 of debt. Their cash inside their SMSF has also risen $238203, so that could be used to pay out their debt, buy another property or invest in some shares or even used to invest in self-funding instalment warrants to buy shares.

In year four James and Cindy decide to continue their strategy and repay the maximum of $50000 each into their super fund to try to repay the debt on their property entirely and boost their super before James maximises his allowable contributions (this will be the last year he is able to contribute $50000 as his super balance will exceed $500000). They repay the remaining $80852 of debt from their superannuation salary sacrifice and the balance from the cash flow from the rent. They also increase their rent to $550 per week or $28600 per annum.

By the end of year four they own their property outright; it is worth $607753; and they are receiving $550 per week rent on the property. Their super fund has increased in value from $400000 to $911397, assuming the remaining initial $200000 in their fund was held in cash at 6 per cent per year.

In addition, at age 55, James and Cindy can each establish a transition to retirement pension, and continue to salary sacrifice or choose to retire if they wish. They could also repeat the process and buy another property if they want to work until age 60, which will also set themselves up with more than $1 million in super. Moreover, if they choose to sell the property once they have established a transition to retirement income stream or an account-based pension at retirement, the property would be free from capital gains tax. Even if they sell before retirement and under the age of 55, they would still pay just 10 per cent capital gains tax (assuming they have owned it for more than 12 months, which they have).

This should illustrate the power of borrowing money inside super and highlight the benefits of repaying debt with income that is only taxed at 15 per cent and capital gains tax at either 15 per cent or as little as 0 per cent. If you are over age 40, this a great strategy for buying property—keeping in mind that you can contribute only $25 000 to super each year while you are under the age of 50 under current legislation (this is likely to be subject to change).

Note that the purchasing costs have been left out of the calculations for the sake of simplicity, so you would need to allow 5 per cent of the purchase value for stamp duty, legal fees and the requisite property searches. These funds need to be available inside the SMSF. In this case, the costs would simply be funded by money in the cash account.

Another point to note is that James would probably reach his maximum contribution level once his member balance inside his super fund exceeded $500 000 in value, which would reduce his maximum contribution to $25 000 a year under the proposed legislation—there is plenty of speculation that these rules will change over time so keep your ear to the ground at budget time (every May) for changes to super laws.

Combine this with a strategy to build a share portfolio to provide liquidity in retirement to pay pensions and you have a very powerful and effective retirement strategy.

Table 7.4 shows how the calculations work for this example.

Table 7.4: benefits of buying property in your SMSF

Year	Super balance	Cash at 6%	Property	Contributions*	Net income†	Debt	End balance
0	$400 000	$200 000	$500 000	$63 750	$(3 500)	$300 000	$400 000
1	$400 000	$212 000	$525 000	$63 750	$2 439	$234 012	$505 427
2	$505 427	$224 720	$551 250	$63 750	$11 746	$159 486	$628 230
3	$628 230	$238 203	$578 813	$63 750	$16 223	$80 852	$752 387
4	$752 387	$252 495	$607 753	$85 000	$23 500	Nil	$911 397

* Contributions are net of 15 per cent contributions tax.
† Includes interest expense at 9 per cent.

Key points

☐ Borrowing in your super fund has been allowed since 2007.

☐ Borrowing can magnify losses as well as gains so caution needs to be exercised when borrowing money in any capacity, but especially within super.

⌘ Seek professional advice when borrowing money inside your SMSF because you are dealing with competing dynamics in terms of the regular superannuation legislation, the specific laws of borrowing within super, your personal financial strategy and your members' attitudes towards risk.

⌘ Self-funding instalment warrants allow you to gear shares in your SMSF.

⌘ Limited recourse loan structures in your SMSF can be an effective way to borrow money to buy property if you are risk tolerant.

⌘ For higher income earners or people who are five or more years away from retirement, borrowing can be a great strategy to boost your asset base in super, so long as you understand that asset values fall as well as rise, and borrowing can magnify both gains and losses.

CHAPTER 8

Risk management and insurance in your fund

I detest Life Insurance agents; they always argue that I shall some day die, which is not so.

Stephen Leacock, Canadian humourist

Australians are heavily under-insured when it comes to personal insurance. According to the Financial Services Council, just 20 per cent of Australians purchase life insurance, and of those who are insured, a large proportion don't have enough insurance to meet their financial obligations in the event of an accident or illness. If you don't have personal insurance then you are a member of one of two possible groups:

¤ those families who are self-insured, meaning they have enough money to meet their financial commitments, such as paying off a mortgage, in the event of accident, illness or death

¤ those who are under-insured, meaning that they, or their families, will not have enough money to continue living comfortably in the event of accident or death.

The average level of insurance is a little over $200000, even though the average person needs around $600000 to continue their lives financially uninterrupted after the loss of income through serious accident, illness or death. It's disturbing enough for a family to grieve over the death or serious illness of a loved one, without the additional problems of trying to carry on without secure finances in place.

Following are some reasons that Australians don't insure themselves or are under-insured, even though many insure their houses, home contents and motor vehicles:

- Insurance can be expensive, particularly if you smoke, are overweight, are aged over 50 or have pre-existing health conditions that increase the risk of a claim being made.

- Life insurance premiums are not tax deductible.

- Australians don't like insurance companies or think their claim may be denied.

- Apathy, or the the 'it won't happen to me' attitude, is prevalent.

- There isn't a system to accurately calculate the amount of insurance necessary to fund your ongoing financial obligations.

- Many already have insurance inside their retail or industry super funds—unfortunately, this is usually nowhere near enough.

Many retirees, or those close to retirement, may not need insurance, as they may be able to self-fund (or self-insure), but if your adult children are members of your fund, or have their own self managed fund, they should have insurance if they are carrying debt, including a mortgage, or have dependants relying on their income or other financial obligations that would continue in the event of accident or death.

Tip

As boring as it may sound, you must read the product disclosure statement from your insurance company, because it gives you a great understanding of the various types of personal insurance.

What personal insurance is available?

There are three main types of insurance and each relates to possible events that may occur in your life that may curtail your financial objectives. They include:

¤ life, and total and permanent disability (TPD) insurance

¤ income protection insurance

¤ trauma insurance.

Life insurance

Life insurance, as the name suggests, allows you to insure your life, or someone else's, against death or the diagnosis of a terminal illness (likely death within 12 months). If the person dies or is diagnosed with a terminal illness, the life insurance company pays out a lump sum to the nominated beneficiaries of the insured. The insured nominates their beneficiary on the insurance application form.

Life insurance premiums payable in your own name are not tax deductible; however, if the policy is owned by your super fund, it will be tax deductible to the SMSF. The other key advantage to owning life insurance inside your super fund is that the premiums are paid by the super fund. This can help your personal cash flow outside the super environment, allowing your superannuation guarantee and salary sacrifice contributions to pay your insurance premiums. Inside an SMSF, you can also ensure that you have a sufficient level of insurance to meet the needs of your beneficiaries given that many commercial super funds have their members heavily under-insured.

Life insurance payments inside super will be tax-free to dependants but will be taxed when they are paid to non-dependants, so if you are aware that your beneficiary is a non-dependant for tax purposes then keep your life insurance outside your SMSF. See the tax calculations and further explanation below.

How much life insurance do I need?

When considering how much life insurance to take out, you will want to consider your liabilities (debts) in addition to a lump sum to provide an income for your beneficiaries to compensate for your lost earnings in the event of death. This may include future payments to take care of household expenses, education, insurance and other living expenses required by your beneficiaries to an age when they can become independent.

For example, if you have a mortgage of $300 000 and have two children who have 10 years of schooling left, at a cost of $10 000 a year, then you may need another $200 000 to supply this income over a 10-year period. That is assuming a 5 per cent return on your $200 000 investment, allowing the income from the capital to supplement your family's income to meet expenses.

Remember, as you accumulate more assets inside or outside of your SMSF, you can reduce the amount of life insurance. So, too, if and when your children become financially independent, you can reduce the size of the insurance policy.

Life insurance premiums increase as the risk of claim increases for the insurance company providing the insurance. Many companies won't insure people over the age of 55, as age is a major contributing factor to the cost of your premiums. Females are cheaper to insure than males as they typically live longer. Smoking, diabetes and obesity are all common ailments that either preclude you from obtaining life insurance or make it so expensive that the premiums are prohibitive. If you have pre-existing conditions, such as injuries, illnesses or disabilities, insurance companies may impose an exclusion for that ailment. That means they will not pay out money for a claim relating to a pre-existing condition.

Most insurance companies require a physical health examination, including blood and urine samples, analysis of medical history, checking your medical records with your doctor, and assessing your weight, height and body mass index, to assess the risk you may pose to making a claim.

My experience

I've had my insurance updated several times, as I've changed the ownership of my insurance from my personal name to my super fund (income protection remains in my personal name), and each time the insurance company sent out a questionnaire to make sure my health had not deteriorated, that my medical records are reflective of this fact and to undertake their own heath checks, including blood and urine tests and a weight check. They send a trained nurse to my house early in the morning to undertake the tests and it doesn't last more than a few minutes. It's simple, fast and easy.

Life insurance payouts inside super

The very nature of life insurance is to help your family in the event of your death, so, like other death benefit payments inside your super fund, life insurance is tax-free to dependants. A dependant is a spouse (including same-sex spouses since 2008) and children under the age of 18. Dependants also include any person who can prove financial dependence upon the deceased. This may include adult children who are financially dependent—for example, living at home and going to university, with fees and living expenses being paid by the deceased. Dependants may also include non-related, non-spouse dependants who have an interdependent relationship with the deceased, such as a family friend who might be receiving financial assistance from the insured.

A life insurance payout made to a non-dependant, however, is taxable. A taxable beneficiary may be a business partner or non-dependent adult child, for example. The amount of tax payable on an insurance payout will depend upon the components of tax-free and taxable amounts within the deceased's account in their super fund, and it is quite a complex calculation.

Calculation of tax on a death benefit paid to a non-dependant

A death benefit to a non-dependant must be paid as a lump sum—only dependants of the deceased can choose to take a pension from a death benefit. That means that life insurance must also be taken as a lump sum and cashed out of the superannuation environment by non-dependants. If a non-dependant receives an insurance death benefit, the insurance payment is paid into the deceased's SMSF free of tax, but the fund must pay tax when it distributes the proceeds of both the insurance payment and the retirement savings in the deceased member's fund balance.

Inside your superannuation you will have taxed and untaxed portions that will depend on the nature of how the money came into the super fund. If you made concessional contributions, such as salary sacrifice, they will make up the taxed elements (a taxed taxable element has already had the tax paid, and the untaxed taxable element has yet to have the tax deducted). The other portion is the tax-free component, which is made up of non-concessional contributions to super that may include any after-tax savings that you contributed from your income, or a windfall, inheritance or money from the sale of an asset. The tax rates are shown in table 8.1.

Table 8.1: rates of tax payable on super benefits paid after the death of a member

Component	Tax rate
Taxable (taxed element)	15% (plus Medicare levy)
Taxable (untaxed element)	30% (plus Medicare levy)
Tax-free	0%

Just to confuse things a little more, a life insurance payment inside your SMSF can create an untaxed element of your taxable component. Typically, this occurs when the deceased has claimed a tax deduction on the insurance premiums or in relation to the future liability to claim benefits. Here is a calculation to help you work out this element and it follows this two-step process:

Step 1: calculating the taxed element

$$\text{Total superannuation lump sum amount} \times \frac{\text{service days}}{\text{service days} + \text{days to retirement}}$$

Service days is the number of days from the deceased member's eligible service date to the date of their death. The eligible service date is the very first day you started contributing to an eligible super fund (not necessarily your current fund if you have rolled money over from previous funds). It is recorded in the member details kept by the fund or shown on the member statement from their SMSF or previous fund; it also appears on super rollover forms from the member's previous fund. If you can't find it, call the fund manager and ask for it. Days to retirement is the number of days from the deceased member's date of death to their retirement age (usually age 65).

Step 2: calculating the untaxed element

The untaxed element is the lump sum amount minus the taxed element and minus the tax-free component.

The following case study will show how this works.

Case study: calculation of the death benefit paid to a non-tax dependant

Leah, age 46, had accumulated superannuation benefits of $700000, of which $500000 is a taxable component (taxed element) and $200000 is a tax-free component. In addition Leah had life insurance of $500000 in her superannuation fund. She has nominated her son Jeremy to receive her superannuation benefit. Jeremy is 22 years old and financially independent, so he is a non-dependant for taxation purposes.

Leah died on 18 September 2010 and her death benefit of $1200000 (consisting of $700000 accumulated balance + $500000 life insurance payout) was paid to her son Jeremy as a lump sum. Leah was born on 14 February 1966 and her eligible service period in superannuation commenced on 10 July 1997.

The amounts of taxed and untaxed elements are calculated as shown below.

Step 1: calculate the taxed element of the taxable component

The taxed element is calculated as the amount generated by the following formula minus any tax-free component (if any, and not below zero):

$$\text{Total superannuation lump sum amount} \times \frac{\text{service days}}{\text{service days} + \text{days to retirement}}$$

$$= \$1.2 \text{ million} \times \frac{4820}{4820 + 7454}$$

$$= \$471\,240$$

(cont'd)

Case study: calculation of the death benefit paid to a non-tax dependant *(cont'd)*

Now let's deduct the tax-free amount:

Taxed element = amount generated above − tax-free component

$$= \$471\,240 - \$200\,000$$

$$= \$271\,240$$

This amount will be taxed at 16.5 per cent.

Step 2: calculate the untaxed element of the taxable component.

Untaxed element = superannuation lump sum benefit − tax free amount − taxed element

$$= \$1.2 \text{ million} - \$271\,240 - \$200\,000$$

$$= \$728\,760$$

This amount will be taxed at 31.5 per cent.

The tax payable on Leah's death benefit is summarised in table 8.2.

Table 8.2: tax payable on death benefit

Component	Amount	Tax rate	Tax payable	Net benefit payable
Tax-free	$200 000	0%	$0	$200 000
Taxable (taxed element)	$271 240	16.5%*	$44 755	$226 485
Taxable (untaxed element)	$728 760	31.5%*	$229 559	$499 201
Total	**$1 200 000**		**$274 314**	**$925 686**

* If Leah's death benefit is paid to her deceased estate and the benefit is passed to Jeremy from her estate, the Medicare levy does not apply. Her estate will withhold 15 per cent tax on the taxed element and 30 per cent tax on untaxed element on the payment made to Jeremy and pay it to the tax office.

Source: © BT Financial Group 2011.

This case study shows that the calculation of the untaxed element of the lump sum death benefit is not limited to the amount of the life insurance in the fund. In Leah's case, the untaxed element of $728 760 is higher than the insurance proceeds of $500 000. The original taxed element was reduced from $500 000 to $271 240 as a result of the recalculation. The alteration of the taxed element becomes less prominent the closer the person gets to age 65. At age 65 (last retirement date) the untaxed element will be reduced to nil.

On a final point, if it is likely that a non-dependant will be a beneficiary of your super, it might be best to leave life insurance outside of your super fund to avoid paying tax altogether. It could be suggested that insurance would be a moot point in any case, as it is really designed to fund dependants in the first instance. Nevertheless, there is no point in paying tax if you know from the beginning that person will be a non-dependant, as is the case with a business partner (key person insurance) or siblings who may have a financial interest (such as a jointly held property with borrowing) in the insured's affairs.

Total and permanent disability insurance

Often coupled with life insurance, total and permanent disability (TPD) insurance is paid as a lump sum to beneficiaries on the diagnosis of a total and permanent disability. This insurance can be held in the name of any entity and, as with life insurance, the premiums are tax deductible to your SMSF. If you were severely incapacitated, you would still have financial obligations that need to be met and TPD insurance ensures you can meet those commitments.

I recommend that you take out the same level of TPD cover as your life insurance policy as they both use the same calculation in determining how much money you would need in the event of a claim. For example, you would still need to clear the mortgage, put the kids through school and meet your normal living expenses for groceries, utilities and other expenses to avoid financial hardship for your family.

In the event of a claim, the lump sum is paid to the insured. In the event that it is an SMSF then it will remain tax-free to dependants and will be taxed similarly to life insurance if it is paid to non-dependants.

The same risk factors considered in the calculation of premiums on life insurance also apply to the calculation of TPD insurance premiums, including age, sex, smoking status, pre-existing ailments and health history.

Income protection insurance

Question: What's your biggest asset?

Answer: You ability to earn an income.

Income protection (sometimes also called disability or temporary disability insurance) is one of the most important forms of insurance. In the event that you cannot work because of incapacity, illness or injury, your policy will pay you 75 per cent of your income. If a claim is made, the payment is taxed as normal income. One key advantage of holding income protection insurance outside your super is that premiums are tax deductible to individuals for all policies. In the case of SMSFs, the premiums are also tax deductible for policies not exceeding two years' worth of payments.

The cost of premiums will vary depending on the level of income you are insuring, the waiting period before a payment is made by the insurer in the event of a claim (30, 60, 90 or 180 days, one year, two years), and the industry in which you work. Certain industries will be more costly to insure, for instance mining.

I often recommend clients, especially higher income earners, to keep income protection outside super and put life and TPD insurance inside super owing to the tax deductibility of income protection premiums and the fact that you can insure to have a claim payable to age 65 for policies held outside of super, rather than the two years of payments possible for policies held inside super.

> **Tip**
>
> Most people prefer to own income protection outside their SMSF because the premiums are then tax deductible and you can receive your payments payable to age 65 in the event that you are unable to work ever again. Super funds only get deductions for income protection payable for up to two years.

Trauma insurance

Trauma insurance is paid as a lump sum in the event of the insured experiencing certain types of traumatic events, such as some cancers, heart attack, stroke or even if you need transplant surgery or contract other serious illnesses. Trauma insurance is designed to cover the costs of treatment and rehabilitation for such illnesses, as they can add up very quickly. Your sick leave may not be enough to cover your expenses, let alone the medical and rehabilitation costs.

Trauma insurance can sit inside your SMSF, but the premiums will not be tax deductible and it is unlikely that you will be able to access a payment in the event of a claim, as that may contravene the conditions of release rules, as you may not be permanently disabled. In the tax office's own words, a trauma claim is not for 'death or disability benefits'. On this basis, you would be better served by owning your trauma insurance in your own name and not in your SMSF.

Trauma can be expensive and the policy can exclude many illnesses (such as certain types of cancers), so make sure you read the product disclosure statement from your insurance company to help you understand how these policies work and what exclusions apply.

In the event of a claim, assuming you recover, many insurance companies will reinsure you. In the event of death, many companies will pay a nominal amount, say $10000, to your beneficiaries. Your premiums will depend on your risk factors and as with other forms of insurance, there may be restrictions, loadings and exclusions that you need to be aware of depending upon your personal risk factors.

> **Tip**
> Make sure you read the product disclosure statement closely to understand the exclusions on trauma insurance—they can be extensive.

Key points

◻ Australians in general are heavily under-insured, so you should assess your family's requirements for all types of insurance and weigh up the cost. You insure your house and your car, so why not insure yourself?

◻ Life insurance covers your life and pays a lump sum to beneficiaries in the event of the death of the insured person. Premiums are tax deductible to your SMSF and payments are tax-free to dependants and taxable to non-dependants. Premiums are not tax deductible outside super.

◻ Total and permanent disability (TPD) insurance provides a lump sum if the insured is totally and permanently disabled. Premiums are tax deductible for your SMSF, but not outside super.

◻ Income protection insurance is tax deductible for up to two years coverage in your SMSF. It will pay you up to 75 per cent of your normal income if a claim is made. The payments are fully taxable in your own name at your marginal tax rate, but premiums are tax deductible for policies that have a claim period of up to two years in your SMSF. Premiums are tax deductible if you hold a trauma policy outside super and you can be covered up to age 65.

◻ Trauma insurance provides a lump sum payment for serious illness and is not tax deductible to the super fund.

Pre-retirement planning and dealing with redundancy

CHAPTER 9

The question isn't at what age I want to retire, it's at what income.
George Foreman, boxer

Pre-retirement planning is an important and exciting process as you prepare for the next stage of your life. Hopefully, you have been busy accumulating enough money to fund your retirement, but if you haven't, there is still plenty of time. Recent statistics indicate that the fastest growing area of work participation is in the over-65 age bracket as more Australians reach Age Pension age without having enough money to live on. Many people have concluded that they are better off working than retiring on the Age Pension. Others are not yet ready to let go of the social aspects that work provides. As a nation we are living longer, we are healthier than ever, and many people simply enjoy working so they keep working well into their 70s. The best part of planning for retirement is that the decision on timing is entirely up to you!

Work is a chore for others and they can't possibly imagine working past age 55. Grey nomads have taken over the nation's highways as caravan parks fill as the colder states begin to cool down in May or June and the dry season arrives in the northern half of Australia. The mass migration continues for another season and the numbers of retiring Australians increase as our ageing workforce says goodbye to the nine to five drone and hello to freedom. Not since leaving school have you experienced such freedom and the opportunities afforded to you in retirement are well worth celebrating.

That is, of course, unless your kids are still at home. The secret here is to stop feeding them and doing their laundry, and they will soon find more accommodating digs. In all seriousness, having children at home can be a financial drain, and with house prices in Australia among the highest in the world, first-home buyers have to save more for longer or else they will need help from you. Couple this with adult children who study for a number of degrees or have a few years off before studying, and many young adults don't leave home until their mid to late 20s, which may be preventing you from either retiring or hitting the nation's highways.

The importance of pre-retirement planning

Whatever your situation or whatever age you decide to retire, pre-retirement planning is essential to ensure a smooth transition from the workforce to retirement. Even if you decide to keep on working, there will be opportunities to use superannuation strategies to reduce income tax, eliminate superannuation tax, and boost your super balance and investments. So don't think pre-retirement is just for those pulling the plug on the workforce: you can access the increasing benefits afforded to the superannuation system to put more money in your pocket.

Here are some benefits of pre-retirement planning that we will be looking at throughout this chapter:

¤   From age 50, you can increase concessional super contributions from $25 000 to $50 000 per year.

¤   From age 55, you can access a transition to retirement income stream to reduce income tax and boost your super, or even retire entirely if you can afford it and don't want to work any more.

¤ At age 60 all superannuation is tax-free if you have retired and cash money out of super or withdraw money in the form of a pension.

¤ From age 65, you have full access to your super, even if you are still working.

¤ Up to age 75 (from 1 July 2013, currently age 70), employers have to make superannuation guarantee (SG) contributions on your behalf. It is proposed at the time of writing that the government will lift age restrictions to allow all employees to be eligible for the SG, and that it will rise from 9 per cent to 12 per cent between 2013 and 2019.

¤ Over the age of 65, if you want to contribute tax-deductible contributions to super, you will need to work at least 40 hours in any consecutive 30-day period each year.

Tip

Pre-retirement is your last real chance to boost your super and retirement savings. Fortunately, it's also the time when superannuation legislation can be used to its greatest advantage.

What is retirement?

Before you look into strategies to boost your retirement savings, you need to understand how retirement is defined. There are a lot confusing rules and regulations around retirement and this is only confused by what I call barbecue advice—people giving you advice with the best intentions but only part knowledge.

Retirement occurs when you stop working and have no intention of returning to work. Even then, you may work for up to 10 hours a week and still be classified as retired. You must also meet a condition of release (see chapter 1) if you want to access your superannuation money. Under the current rules, if you were born before 1 July 1960 you must be 55 years of age or over to retire and get access to your super. If you were born between 1 July 1960 and June 30 1964, then your preservation age will depend upon your birth date (see table 9.1, overleaf). For everyone born after 30 June 1964, preservation age is 60.

Table 9.1: preservation ages

Date of birth	Preservation age
Before 1 July 1960	55
1 July 1960 – 30 June 1961	56
1 July 1961 – 30 June 1962	57
1 July 1962 – 30 June 1963	58
1 July 1963 – 30 June 1964	59
From 1 July 1964	60

Source: <www.ato.gov.au>.

To reiterate, you must have the genuine intention to retire and not return to the workforce at the time of making your declaration of retirement and if you are still working, your work hours must be less than 10 hours per week. You must sign a declaration of retirement to indicate and acknowledge that you have met a condition of release and can therefore access your superannuation as either a pension or a lump sum. This declaration forms the minutes and records for the legitimate maintenance of your fund and does not have to be sent to the ATO. It is simply best practice to acknowledge a condition of release and the genuine intention not to work again.

I have heard clients trying to second-guess the system by saying that they heard retirement was working 20 hours or fewer, but this is a confusion with the age at which people can access a state-based Seniors Card. These are available to you if you work less than 20 hours per week and are over the age of 60.

Once you are reach the age of 65, you have met another condition of release and you are eligible to access your superannuation whether you are working or not. Over-65s, can work full time and still have access to their superannuation as an income stream or lump sum. By age 65 you do not need to use a transition to retirement income stream (see p. 152) because you have met this full condition of release. Transition to retirement income streams are only for those aged 55 to 64.

You will not be eligible to access a government Age Pension if you retire before the age of 65 (some women may be eligible before age 65). So if you retire at age 61 and you don't quite have enough money to live on, you will not be eligible for the Age Pension until 65. Check the section on the Age Pension in chapter 10 for more details.

What will you do in retirement?

What you do in retirement is entirely up to you. My clients do all sorts of things, ranging from golfing, bowling, swimming, travelling overseas, taking cruises, travelling in a caravan, camping, visiting kids, looking after grandkids, looking after pets, renovating houses, helping kids renovate houses, joining Rotary or Probus, volunteering for charities, and all manner of other activities.

Although many of my clients heading into retirement say they are nervous about what they will do with their time, at their first six-month review they tell me that they don't know how they ever had time to work. In fact, most are not sure how they had the time to work because they are now so busy with other activities that they can't imagine working.

There are plenty of books on retirement and what to do if you are nervous about leaving the workforce. After all, retiring is one of the biggest changes you will experience in life, and many people derive their self-worth and value system from their work, not to mention their social life. So if you are feeling a little insecure about leaving the workforce, I strongly suggest talking to friends and family who have been through the transition or seek professional help from a counsellor or one of the many volunteer organisations that assist with the transition. For example, in Victoria, you could seek assistance from one of the following organisations (noting that some organisations are national, such as Centrelink):

- Centrelink, Tel. 132 490

- Job Network Information Line, Tel. 1300 363 365

- Department of Education, Training and Youth Affairs, Tel. (03) 9920 4777

- Council on the Ageing Victoria, Tel. 1300 135 090

- MoneyHelp, Tel. 1800 149 689.

> **Tip**
>
> Pre-retirement is the single most important time to seek financial advice to see if there is anything you can do to boost your retirement savings. So book a free first appointment with a financial adviser or two and see what they have to offer—make sure the meeting is free and obtain a full schedule of costs if you decide to use their services. Check <www.moneysmart.gov.au> and read the section on how to choose a financial adviser.

When to retire

A very common question I am asked is, 'When should I retire?' The answer has a number of angles to consider, depending on what you are trying to achieve and what your circumstances are. The most common answer is as soon as possible, so long as you have the funds to sustain an income stream that will maintain your standard of living for the rest of your life. Of course, we don't know how long we are going to live, and it's probably best not to know, but lifestyle, genetics and perhaps the life expectancy tables (see table 9.4 on p. 148) may help you figure out how much money you will need in retirement

If you plan to sell assets to make contributions to super, you may be triggering capital gains tax. One of your main objectives will be to reduce capital gains tax, so it is best to sell assets to contribute to super in a year in which your taxable income is at a minimum. You may also want to ensure that your partner's income is also at a minimum if the asset is jointly held. For example, if an investment property is in joint names then the tax liability for capital gains tax will be borne equally by each partner. You may want to retire on 30 June in one financial year and put the property on the market in the next financial year (literally, the next day) to ensure your normal work-based income is zero or as close to zero as possible.

Capital gains tax is not a separate tax. Any taxable earnings you have from capital gains on assets purchased after 20 September 1985 will be added to any other taxable income that you may have. Normal marginal tax rates will then be levied upon you and you will receive a tax bill. So make sure you maximise your concessional contributions to super ($50 000 each if over 50) in that financial year to reduce your capital gains tax bill, as super contributions are not part of your taxable income. You will, however, pay 15 per cent contributions tax, but that is better than 30 per cent, 37 per cent or 45 per cent tax, depending on what your other earnings are. Get advice on how to do this in the most legally tax-effective manner.

Remember, if you are selling a property, the capital gains tax will be payable from the date on which you entered a contract for sale, not the settlement date. This means that the day a contract for sale is exchanged is the date that capital gains tax is levied, so you should exchange contracts in the financial year in which you have the lowest taxable earnings. Simply delaying settlement into another financial year will not help you. Again, people get caught out trying to second-guess the system with barbecue advice, especially when it comes to capital gains tax.

Holidays and long service leave—take it or leave it

Remember, that when you are considering the timing of retirement and what your income will be, you will need to consider the effects of any long service leave and holiday leave you have accrued. In most cases, I recommend that you take this leave before you retire for these reasons:

¤   When you are on leave, you are accumulating more leave.

¤   When you are on leave, you are not only being paid but also accumulating more superannuation guarantee payments from your employer.

¤   You can salary sacrifice your income into super to boost your super further.

This works particularly well when one partner is still working and both people can live off the one income and salary sacrifice a large portion (up to $50 000) of the salary of the person on leave. There is usually income left over to supplement their income, assuming they are earning more than $50 000 per annum. People who have a large amount of long service leave may have the option of working part time and taking half pay for a longer period, thereby reducing work hours in the lead-up to retirement. For others, long service leave may mean three to six months' leave before official retirement (and superannuation drawdown) actually commences.

Planning for retirement and major expenses

Part of your financial planning for retirement should include planning for any lump sum expenses, including paying off any debt. As retirement is usually a tax-free affair, there is no point in heading into retirement with debt. Credit card or store card debt should be paid out entirely; the home mortgage should be paid down; and any investment debt needs some consideration as to why you would want to keep it. If you feel that the potential market forces will push the value of a property or shares higher then there may be reason to hold assets. Otherwise, it is often best to sell the assets and contribute the funds to superannuation to boost your chances of drawing an adequate tax-free income.

It is often better to maximise your contributions to superannuation (i.e. $50 000 each per year) to boost your super and save tax, and then at retirement cash some of the money out of super to repay the mortgage on your own house or even an investment property. The reason for this is that you repay your mortgage with after-tax income—and remember, most people pay 30 per cent, 37 per cent or 45 per cent tax on their income. It is often best to put $50 000 each into super, saving up to 66 per cent in tax, and then at retirement cash out some money to complete repayment of the mortgage. This may be a more tax-effective strategy to eliminate the mortgage.

Other expenses, such as new cars, renovations or caravans, can be taken out of superannuation money once you have met a condition of release. Alternatively, you may have other savings outside of super (perhaps it should be contributed to super as a non-concessional contribution) earmarked for debt reduction or to purchase assets when you retire. For example, you may have a wish list that looks like this:

New 4WD vehicle to tow caravan (diesel)	$50 000
Caravan	$60 000
Bathroom renovation	$20 000
New kitchen	$20 000
Total cash required at retirement	**$150 000**

When you are planning for your retirement, you need to take into account not only the level of assets that you need to produce the income you require to meet your expenses, but also your initial and ongoing capital costs, such as starting retirement with a new car. I always laugh when my 70-year-old dad says every time he buys a new car, 'This car will see me out'.

How much will I need to retire?

There are many factors to consider when trying to calculate how much money you will need in retirement. The objective is to accumulate enough assets to produce the income you need to meet your ongoing expenses and capital costs. The calculation may be further muddied by the fact that the Age Pension is available to most retirees: the upper level of the assets test to determine your eligibility is well over $1 million for a home-owning couple, so you can now have more than $1 million in assets excluding your own home and still receive a part pension (the lower limit for the Age Pension is a little less than $300000 for a home-owning couple, at which point you would receive a full Age Pension—see chapter 10 for an explanation of how the Age Pension works).

I believe most couples need around $1000 per week to meet their expenses and save a few dollars for capital expenses, such as trips away and home repairs and renovations. That being said, I've seen plenty of couples who need $100000 a year, or $2000 per week, to meet their expenses, and several who need $250000 to $300000 a year. The point is, everyone has different standards and expectations when it comes to retirement plans and expenses, so it's important to match your super balance with your expectations.

All too often I meet people who may be used to earning and spending $250000 to $500000 a year but have saved very little towards their retirement. To maintain their standard of living, they will simply have to keep working. They then struggle with the thought of having to save for retirement. It's important to have a savings mentality from early in life, because this makes retirement so much easier.

I generally recommend that you will be able to live comfortably and have enough income for life if you draw between 5 per cent and

7 per cent of your account balance each year. Any more than this and you eat into your capital too quickly and won't have enough to last you if investment markets are unfavourable. Table 9.2 illustrates your level of income, assuming you are age 65 and drawing 5 to 7 per cent of your capital as an income and what level of Age Pension income you could expect, based on the current limits in late 2011 (that are indexed up every March and every September).

I created table 9.2 to show my clients what level of income they could expect given their level of assets. Keep in mind that we have clients with many millions and clients with just a few hundred thousand, so this scale could go to $5 to 10 million, but most clients with more than $2 million in assets are quite comfortable with their income. The table might help you work out how much super you will need to retire.

Table 9.2: approximate amount of retirement income based on assets

Super balance	5% drawdown	to	7% drawdown	Approx. Age Pension*	Maximum total income
$300 000	$15 000		$21 000	$27 976	$48 976
$400 000	$20 000		$28 000	$24 076	$52 076
$500 000	$25 000		$35 000	$20 176	$55 176
$600 000	$30 000		$42 000	$16 276	$58 276
$700 000	$35 000		$49 000	$12 376	$61 376
$800 000	$40 000		$56 000	$8 476	$64 476
$900 000	$45 000		$63 000	$4 589	$67 589
$1 000 000	$50 000		$70 000	$689	$70 689
$1 100 000	$55 000		$77 000	$0	$77 000
$1 200 000	$60 000		$84 000	$0	$84 000
$1 300 000	$65 000		$91 000	$0	$91 000
$1 400 000	$70 000		$98 000	$0	$98 000
$1 500 000	$75 000		$105 000	$0	$105 000

* Age Pension amount is based upon a home-owning couple, assuming their combined super balance is their only asset excluding their own home. It is also indexed up every March and September. Amounts will be different for singles and non-home-owners. Age Pension figures valid as at 20 September 2011.

What will your life be like in retirement?

The ASFA Retirement Standard is the result of a regular survey by Westpac and the Association of Superannuation Funds Australia (ASFA) that illustrates how much income singles and couples need for a modest and a comfortable retirement. It is based on surveys of current retiree expenses, so it provides a great benchmark for indicating how much the average person needs in retirement (see table 9.3). As you can see, a single female wanting a modest lifestyle in retirement needs $21 746 a year; a couple happy with a modest lifestyle need $31 519 a year; a single with a comfortable lifestyle needs $40 121 a year; and a couple, $54 954.

Table 9.3: the cost of a modest and comfortable lifestyle

Expense	Modest lifestyle (single)	Modest lifestyle (couple)	Comfortable lifestyle (single)	Comfortable lifestyle (couple)
Housing — ongoing only	$56.91	$54.63	$65.96	$76.46
Energy	$31.71	$42.11	$32.18	$43.64
Food	$75.93	$157.28	$108.47	$195.24
Clothing	$17.92	$29.09	$38.79	$58.18
Household goods and services	$26.00	$35.25	$73.13	$85.67
Health	$35.10	$67.75	$69.65	$122.92
Transport	$92.10	$94.71	$137.25	$139.86
Leisure	$72.18	$107.53	$218.72	$299.73
Communications	$9.21	$16.12	$25.30	$32.21
Total per week	$417.05	$604.47	$769.44	$1 053.91
Total per year	**$21 746.00**	**$31 519.00**	**$40 121.00**	**$54 954.00**

Source: Reproduced with permission from the Association of Superannuation Funds of Australia.

The Westpac–ASFA numbers are consistent with my figures shown in table 9.2 and the two tables combined may help you calculate a more accurate retirement sum. Of course, at the end of the day, you will live off what you have saved plus any Age Pension you are entitled to. Most people live up to their expectations and within their means, as they can only spend what they have.

The only other factor you may want to consider is your life expectancy. We used to use these life expectancy tables in the financial planning industry all the time when calculating allocated pensions and term allocated pensions, but these days they are really just a guideline to provide people with an idea of how long they can expect to live at a particular age. I'm showing you these really just as a matter of interest as I don't know, and you don't know, how long you will live. I do hope your money outlives you. Table 9.4 shows life expectancy from different ages, for example, at 65 in 2007–09, a woman still has 21.8 years to live. As I always say to my clients, if I do a good job, your biggest problem will be an estate-planning problem.

Table 9.4: life expectancy (additional years of life at selected ages) for Australians, 1881–2009

Years	Males				Females			
	at 0	at 25	at 45	at 65	at 0	at 25	at 45	at 65
1881–1890	47.2	37.1	23.0	11.1	50.8	39.7	25.6	12.3
1891–1900	51.1	38.9	24.0	11.3	54.8	41.7	26.7	12.8
1901–1910	55.2	40.6	24.8	11.3	58.8	43.4	27.6	12.9
1920–1922	59.2	42.7	26.0	12.0	63.3	45.7	29.0	13.6
1932–1934	63.5	44.4	26.9	12.4	67.1	47.2	29.7	14.2
1946–1948	66.1	45.0	26.8	12.3	70.6	48.7	30.5	14.4
1953–1955	67.1	45.5	27.2	12.3	72.8	50.2	31.4	15.0
1965–1967	67.6	45.4	27.0	12.2	74.2	51.2	32.3	15.7
1975–1977	69.6	46.9	28.3	13.1	76.6	53.1	34.0	17.1
1985–1987	72.7	49.5	30.8	14.6	79.2	55.4	36.1	18.6
1995–1997	75.6	51.8	33.1	16.1	81.3	57.1	37.7	19.8
2004–2006	78.7	54.7	35.7	18.3	83.5	59.2	39.7	21.5
2007–2009	79.3	55.2	36.3	18.7	83.9	59.5	40.1	21.8

Source: Australian Social Trends, ABS Catalogue No. 4102.0, March 2011, p. 2, Australian Bureau of Statistics.

Structuring your investments for retirement

As you're heading towards retirement, you may want to think about restructuring your investments to ensure you are well positioned to maximise your cash flow and minimise your tax. I'm forever trying to unwind gearing strategies sold to clients by property spruikers as the strategy is just not appropriate for retirees or pre-retirees (those over 50). Gearing will only delay retirement. In addition, the after-tax cash flow on most residential property is below 4 per cent, so when that poor cash flow is combined with high debt, the so-called investment is actually a liability.

As I mentioned earlier, I often say, 'Property for wealth creation and shares for retirement'. While many people don't like the volatility of shares (they can have more cash in their portfolio), shares don't have high holding costs like properties do. Retirees also need larger proportions of cash in their super fund to pay account-based pensions.

Buying properties in your 50s to make a quick buck before you retire can be catastrophic to retirement plans if you buy the wrong property. Property does not automatically rise in value, as many people who bought investment properties in Queensland in the past 10 years have discovered.

If properties need to be sold to reduce debt and increase cash holdings, capital gains tax is triggered and you might need to consider the timing of the property sale, how to maximise your super contributions to reduce tax liabilities and how much income tax (including capital gains tax) you will have to pay. The key objective here is to maximise super and minimise tax.

Try to sell a property in a year in which you have low taxable income and maximise your super concessional contributions (you can contribute up to $50 000 each per year) to reduce your taxable income. You can also make non-concessional contributions (up to $450 000 tax-free each in a three-year period) into super to boost your super balances. You can then buy new income-producing assets that will produce high tax-free income, which may include term deposits, shares, managed funds or ASX-listed property securities.

Increasing cash to pay pensions

You will need to hold enough cash in your super fund to pay pensions once you retire. This is particularly important for people who have property in their super fund, as often the net income (after expenses) from that property will not be sufficient to pay the minimum account-based pension. If you do not have enough cash in your fund to pay pensions, you will need to sell assets to fund your income stream and this might require that you sell a property inside your fund to pay pensions.

Your investment strategy should specify how you plan to meet the cash flow requirements of pensions when a member retires. Apart from risk management, diversification of investments might allow members to have enough cash to fund pensions, assuming you have some high–income producing assets, such as fixed interest investments or commercial property, which typically produces a higher income than residential (although they can have more risk, for instance, in obtaining a tenant).

Tips to boost your super before retirement

Here are some ideas to help you increase your super in the years when you are approaching retirement.

◻ Salary sacrifice your maximum concessional contributions to super ($50 000 per year) for over-50s or $25 000 for under-50s.

◻ Take advantage of the government's co-contribution if you earn less than $62 000 per year (exactly $61 920), as you could get a tax-free contribution from the government of up to $1000 (the legislation is changing at the time of writing — see chapter 12 for more information).

◻ Salary sacrifice into your partner's account to boost their super balance (assuming you meet the normal contribution limits).

◻ If your partner has a low super balance and you sell an asset, it makes sense to make a larger non-concessional contribution in their name to boost their super.

◻ If, as it has proposed, the government legislates to permit concessional contributions to super of up to $50 000 a year if a member's fund balance is less than $500 000, you will be able to take advantage of this rule to boost a partner's low-balance account. (See <www.samhenderson.com.au> for changes to legislation and how it affects you.)

¤ Once you are over the age of 45, buy assets inside rather than outside super—they will be free of capital gains tax at retirement if you sell them.

¤ Rather than paying off the mortgage, maximise your salary sacrifice (concessional) contributions to super to reduce your income tax. At retirement, cash out the money to pay off the mortgage.

Redundancy

If you are made redundant from your job, it can be a very stressful and insecure time, but it can be a real godsend if it happens just before you want to retire. It can give you a windfall if you have worked at the same place for a long time. However, redundancy must be a bona fide or genuine redundancy for your redundancy payment to qualify for the tax benefits.

Much of a redundancy payout is tax-free and can be contributed to super as a large non-concessional (no tax) contribution. Let's look at an example.

Let's assume someone has worked at the same company for 32 years and they get three weeks' pay for every year of service. Their payout would be something like this:

$32 \times 3 = 96$ weeks @ $1600 per week = $153600.

To calculate the amount of your redundancy payment that will be tax-free, you use the figures supplied for each tax year on the ATO website. The first $8435 (base limit) of the redundancy payment is tax-free, in addition to $4218 for each year of service (see table 9.5, overleaf). Everyone gets the base limit tax-free, no matter how long they have worked somewhere, and then they add an additional $4218 for each year of service. For the example above, we would take the base rate of $8435 plus $32 \times \$4218 = \$143411$.

That means that $143411 of the total payout of $153600 will be tax-free.

The remaining $10198 would be taxed at just 15 per cent—and that rate applies up to a level of $165000, and top marginal tax rates apply thereafter.

Your long service leave and holiday pay would be taxed at 31.5 per cent (unless you were employed before 1978, in which case 5 per cent of your long service and holiday pay would be taxed at your marginal rates).

If you are offered redundancy, you should get advice from a qualified financial adviser who has experience in redundancy, as they can save you thousands of dollars by providing good advice.

Table 9.5: tax-free amount in redundancy payments, 2011–12

Income year	Base limit	For each complete year of service
2011–12	$8435	$4218

Source: <www.ato.gov.au>.

Transition to retirement income stream

You can start a transition to retirement income stream (TRIS) once you reach age 55, and continue to receive it to age 65 (when you will be eligible to take your super without any restrictions). TRIS is a non-commutable income stream, which means you cannot make lump sum withdrawals from the fund. You must draw down at least 4 per cent (3 per cent in 2012 financial year) or up to 10 per cent of your superannuation balance per year as regular payments (that is, between 3 and 10 per cent in 2011–12). Most people take the income stream in the form of monthly payments, but it can also be taken as a single payment each year.

Setting up a TRIS can be a handy way to boost your super. The TRIS payments subsidise your usual income while you increase or start salary sacrificing into your super fund up to the annual limit of $50000.

You may also want to establish a TRIS in order to reduce your work hours and maintain your income; for example, you might want to work part time and draw some income from your super.

Importantly, before setting up a TRIS you must ensure that your SMSF trust deed allows for this kind of income stream. If not, you will need to update your trust deed (a cost of about $500).

A TRIS offers the same benefits of an account-based pension. That means once you reach age 60 the income is tax-free, and concessionally taxed for those aged 55 to 59. In addition, no capital gains tax and no earnings tax will we levied for assets held inside your TRIS account. Even if you don't need the income and could still afford to salary sacrifice the full $50 000 each year, there may still be tax advantages in establishing a TRIS.

If your spouse has a low super balance, it may be possible to establish a TRIS and re-contribute the TRIS income as a non-concessional contribution to their account and also salary sacrifice the concessional contributions into their account. This may be a major benefit to avoid the $500 000 benchmark at which your concessional contributions will be limited to $25 000 if your balance exceeds $500 000 (proposed legislation in late 2011).

Another good reason for establishing a TRIS is if you want to sell an asset inside your fund that may normally attract capital gains tax (CGT). Once an account in a super fund is used to pay an income stream, its earnings are tax-free, and no CGT will be charged if an asset in that account is sold. If you want to sell an asset free of CGT, then a TRIS offers a tax-free method.

The income drawn out of a TRIS is also concessionally taxed. For those aged 60 and over, it is tax-free. For those aged 55 to 59 the non-taxable portion of their income is tax-free and the taxable portion is taxed at their normal marginal tax rate. The TRIS also attracts a 15 per cent tax rebate, ensuring that the maximum tax payable is just 31.5 per cent (including the Medicare levy).

Let's look at an example. Let's say you have a $400 000 balance in your SMSF member account and $350 000 is taxable and $50 000 is non-taxable (check your member statement in your tax return if you're not sure, but this amount comes from your non-concessional contributions). The portion of the income that relates to the taxable component ($350 000) will be taxed at your normal marginal tax rate but you will also receive a rebate of 15 per cent to reduce that tax (to nil for many people). The portion of the income stream derived from the non-taxable portion of your super balance ($50 000) remains tax-free.

So if you draw the minimum of 4 per cent of the account balance at 1 July, you would be drawing $16 000 per year. Given $50 000 of the $400 000 is tax-free, that equates to 12.5 per cent, or $2000, of the

$16000. The balance of $14000 is fully taxable. If you earn less than $80000 but more than $37000 in total including the TRIS, you would pay $4800 (30 per cent) in income tax. However, you would receive 15 per cent tax rebate, which would reduce your tax by $2100 to $2700.

In addition, the fund's investment income and capital gains tax would be nil for the year for any assets sitting within the pension account.

Tip

See my website for a sample member statement for either an SMSF or a retail super fund to see what your superannuation components look like in a real-life document.

Case study: transition to retirement

Anna has $350000 in her super fund, $100000 of which is an untaxed portion. She commences a TRIS while salary sacrificing $25000 per year from her regular income from her job and draws enough from her TRIS to ensure her cash flow is exactly the same. So she feels no pain—this is an important point because the moment you mention savings to people they immediately think of giving up their comforts and inertia sets in. So, she would be drawing $20950 per year or around 6 per cent of her account balance. The minimum she can take is $14000 (4 per cent) a year and the maximum Anna can take is $35000 a year (10 per cent). Table 9.6 compares doing nothing with implementing a TRIS strategy.

Table 9.6: doing nothing versus TRIS strategy

	Do nothing	Implement strategy
Gross income	$76000	$71950
Tax payable	$17490	$13432
Net income	$58510	$58518
Super balance	$377046	$22745
Pension balance	—	$360390
Net balance year 1	$377046	$383135
Balance at 65	$720248	$821584

Note: The calculations assume investment return of 7 per cent; salary increasing at 4 per cent a year; and excess income will not be reinvested.

The benefit of this strategy, compared with doing nothing (current) over 10 years, is shown in figure 9.1.

Figure 9.1: benefit of a TRIS

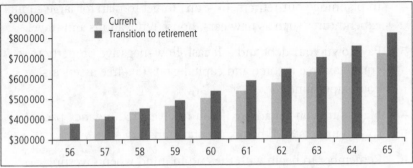

In this example, Anna will be $101 336 better off at retirement. Can you imagine if she salary sacrificed the full $50 000 into her super until she hit $500 000 and withdrew the minimum? With her $101 336 benefit she would still be better of at age 65 by $100 per week, assuming she drew 5 per cent of her balance as an account-based pension, and she feels no pain in terms of cash flow as it remains the same. Her fund pays no earnings tax and no capital gains tax on her pension account. A TRIS is a no brainer!

Source: © BT Financial Group 2011.

Tip

I have met very few people who do not benefit from the many advantages of a transition to retirement income stream (TRIS). So check your trust deed to ensure it allows for a TRIS (update it if necessary) and seek advice if you need to, but if you are aged 55 to 64, you really need to consider starting a TRIS.

Key points

¤ Retirement is officially classified as being over age 55 (60 if born after July 1964) and working less than 10 hours a week.

¤ The average couple needs a little more than $1000 per week or $52 000 per annum and the average single needs a bit over $40 000 for a comfortable retirement.

¤   Remember to check your eligibility for an Age Pension at age 65 when you are calculating how much money you need for retirement.

¤   In planning your retirement, don't forget to plan for large capital expenditures such as new cars, house renovations and travel.

¤   Pay down your debt and sell cash flow–negative property to create tax-free income and capital gains tax–free assets inside your super fund.

¤   Make sure you get advice if you receive a redundancy package so you understand the tax ramifications.

¤   Remember to begin with the end in mind when investing, so consider buying assets in super to avoid having to sell them later to fund retirement.

¤   Remember to build up cash or income-producing assets, such as shares, to pay pensions in retirement. Illiquid assets, such as property, can be a hindrance when your SMSF is paying pensions.

¤   Salary sacrifice will boost your super.

¤   Transition to retirement income stream will boost your super and reduce your income tax.

¤   Seek advice in your pre-retirement phase because legislation is constantly changing and it's such an important process. Visit <www.samhenderson.com.au> for advice if you need it or speak to your accountant or financial adviser.

CHAPTER 10

Retirement and how to eliminate tax forever

Retirement at sixty-five is ridiculous. When I was sixty-five I still had pimples.

George Burns, US comedian

So, you have arrived. But before you can go away and relax, you have a whole bunch of questions to deal with before the celebrations begin. You will need to know how to set up an income stream for your SMSF, how often you can draw your income and how much you should draw. You may also want to know what to do if only one partner has retired and the other is still working, and whether you can go back to work if retirement isn't for you or if you get a job offer.

Fortunately, despite its complexities, the Australian superannuation system affords you a great deal of flexibility at retirement, and this fact, coupled with an SMSF structure for your super, means you have one of the most malleable investment structures available to anyone anywhere on the globe. You can increase income, change the frequency of your payments, withdraw lump sums—heck, you can even withdraw the whole lot if you want, and tax-free if you are over the age of 60. You can stop your account-based pension; you can restart it; you can make more super contributions up to age 65 (though in another account); and you can invest in an environment that is free of capital gains tax, income tax and investment earnings tax.

It simply doesn't get any better. A number of possible income streams may be available to you, but your main objective will be to maximise your income and minimise your tax while protecting your lump sum—everyone has the same needs here, though people have different attitudes to risk and different asset allocations and investment preferences. But this is the beauty of an SMSF and the flexibility and control it provides.

Can I go back to work after I retire?

Oddly enough, before signing their retirement declaration many clients ask me if they can go back to work after they retire if they want to. I think they picture themselves sitting around watching TV and getting bored, but in my experience of dealing with hundreds of retirees, I have rarely seen anyone bored in retirement. There have been a few, and they have returned to work after 6 to 12 months, but the vast majority have taken to retirement like fish to water.

The declaration of retirement that you sign for the minutes of your SMSF should simply state that you have the genuine intention to cease work (doing less than 10 hours work per week) at the time of signing and that you have met a condition of release, namely reached the age of at least 55. Talk to your adviser or administrator about this process and to produce the necessary forms. You can go back to work at any time, but a couple of pieces of legislation exist that have been designed to stop you from gaining an advantage by deceit. The first one refers to early access to your superannuation, and another aims to ensure you are not establishing a scheme to evade tax.

The *Superannuation Industry (Supervision) Act 1993* details the conditions of release and the definition of retirement. If you are simply trying to access your super without retiring, then you could very well land yourself in hot water for using an early-release super scheme. Of course, you wouldn't be the only who has tried this strategy, and there is little doubt the result would end in the same way: fines, jail and penalties. It's not pretty.

Part IVA of the *Income Tax Assessment Act 1936* (Tax Act) outlines the general principles behind the notion that a taxpayer cannot set up a scheme to avoid tax. The Act includes a very broad statement that simply says that you cannot establish a scheme to avoid tax. This includes superannuation and early release schemes that could allow the taxpayer to reduce or eliminate tax by saying they are retiring and then going straight back to work.

Can I contribute to super if I retire?

As discussed in chapter 1, it is possible to retire before you reach the age of 65 and also still make contributions until age 65. Under the definition of work, those who earn income and therefore want to make contributions to super (concessional or non-concessional) are deemed to be self-employed. This includes cases of people selling assets such as property and wanting to reduce capital gains tax by making concessional contributions to super (up to $50000) to reduce their taxable income and therefore reduce or eliminate their capital gain tax liability. You may also make non-concessional contributions up to the limit of $150000 per year or use the three-year averaging provision to make a $450000 contribution. It is also possible to make the $450000 contribution the day before you turn 65.

For people who own properties in joint names and sell them, then it is possible to use the above strategy for each partner, allowing you to put $1000000 into super from the sale of a property or another asset, consisting of $50000 each as a concessional contribution and $450000 each as non-concessional contributions. This highlights the importance of knowing how the superannuation system works in Australia and how to optimise your opportunities.

What is the work test?

Once you are over age 65, however, you need to pass the work test in order to be allowed to contribute to super. You do not need to meet the work test if you are under 65.

The work test rules stipulate that to be eligible to make a contribution to super if you are aged 65, you need to work 40 hours in any 30-day consecutive period in the financial year in which you want to make the contributions. In other words, you need to work at least one week in any month in the year. As you can probably imagine, I have had my fair share of retirees doing 'filing in the office' to try to satisfy the work test, but often it's highly advantageous to gain employment for the benefit of reducing tax and boosting your retirement savings within super.

However, once you are over age 65, you are no longer eligible to use the three-year averaging provision that allows you to put $450 000 into super as a non-concessional contribution. You are limited to $150 000 of non-concessional and $50 000 of concessional contributions per person per year. There is nothing stopping you from working for two weeks from the last week in June to the end of the first week in July and making a $150 000 contribution in each week to achieve a total $300 000 contribution, so long as you operate within the realms of the law. This spreads the contributions over two financial years and still allows you to meet the work test and maximise contributions of up to $400 000.

Keep in mind that the work needs to be legitimate paid employment, for which you receive an employment declaration and a pay slip. It does not mean you can do some baby sitting, property renovation or your own administration work. You need to be able to prove to the tax office that you completed at least 40 hours of genuine paid employment in the year.

> **Tip**
>
> To satisfy the work test, you must have genuine paid employment, and proof of payment, which needs to include a pay slip. It does not allow for working on an investment property or baby sitting for the grandchildren.

Types of retirement benefits

Over the years a myriad of different retirement income streams have been available as superannuation legislation has changed, such as allocated pensions, term allocated pensions and defined benefit pensions. If you have any issues with past types of pensions, particularly term allocated pensions, seek immediate advice about your options.

However, at the time of writing, the two main income streams that an SMSF would want to establish are:

¤   transition to retirement income stream

¤   account-based pension.

Outside your SMSF, you may have other income stream options, such as pensions offered through defined benefit super plans. Defined benefit plans are commonly available to state or Commonwealth government employers who entered the public service some time ago and joined old schemes that gave them a guaranteed and indexed income stream for life once they retired. Others are lump sum schemes that pay the beneficiary a multiple of the last three years salary on retirement, without a pension option. In this case, members have to cash out the money or, better still, roll it over into another super scheme like an SMSF.

Examples of defined benefit pensions may include state government super schemes, such as the State Superannnuation Scheme of New South Wales (SSS), and ComSuper, which administers the various Commonwealth government super schemes, including the Common-wealth Superannuation Scheme (CSS), the Public Sector Superannuation Scheme (PSS) and Military Super. Many companies also offered defined benefit schemes in the past and will have employees and pensioners still benefiting from these super schemes. But defined benefit schemes have been phased out for all new employees by both government and the private sector, and existing schemes have been trying to move people out of them for years. Why? Because they are too good to be true, that's why. If you have benefits in one of these schemes, it's unlikely that you should get out of it, but seek advice from a good financial adviser, and beware of those who tell you to get out of a defined benefit scheme so they can manage your money and earn a fee from you—that is unlikely to be the best long-term solution for you.

The Age Pension, paid through Centrelink, is another non–SMSF income stream.

We looked at transition to retirement income streams (TRIS) in chapter 9, because these are pre-retirement income streams. That leaves the most common type of income stream to discuss now—the account-based pension.

About income streams

Most people in retirement will have a combination of income streams from money held outside of their SMSF, invested in their own name, their SMSF pension, perhaps a defined benefit pension, and possibly even an Age Pension from Centrelink if they are eligible.

Account-based pensions

An account-based pension is simply a retirement income stream established with money from superannuation. It is not a product that you buy from someone. In fact, it is almost as easy as just setting up a direct debit from your super fund's bank account to your personal bank account. That being said, there is a proper process to follow, but it is relatively simple.

What you should know about account-based pensions

Here are some of the rules and benefits of account-based pensions:

- You must reach a condition of release to commence an account-based pension.
- You pay no lump sum taxes when you roll your super benefits into an account-based pension from the accumulation mode in your SMSF.
- You have flexibility in how you can draw your income, but you must take the minimum amount required at least once a year.
- You have plenty of choice in investment products to support payment of your pension.
- You can make lump sum withdrawals from your pension account at any time (unlike a TRIS).
- The account-based pension is highly tax effective: you pay no capital gains tax and no earnings tax on investments in the pension account.

¤ You can nominate dependent reversionary beneficiaries who will receive tax-effective pensions in the event of your death.

¤ You will pay no income tax on the income from your account-based pension once you reach the age of 60.

> **Tip**
>
> Account-based pensions are the single best structure under which to invest your assets, because no income tax is deducted once you reach age 60, and no earnings tax or capital gains tax are payable either. This is why it's smart to pump money into the superannuation environment and why super is such a good investment structure.

You must draw a minimum amount from your pension, depending on your age. Over the past few years, the government has permitted a discount to these minimums because of the way the GFC affected retirees' investments. The theory behind this was to allow retirement balances to recover while people drew less from their fund. For instance, a person aged 55 to 65 normally has to draw a minimum of 4 per cent; however in the 2011–12 financial year they were permitted a discount of 25 per cent and in 2010–11, they were permitted a 50 per cent discount, so the minimums were 2 per cent and 3 per cent respectively for 55 to 64 year olds.

There is no upper limit on the amount that you can draw. The previous super pension, an allocated pension, did have a maximum amount set, based upon a pension valuation factor, but these days there is no maximum, only a minimum. The minimums are shown in table 10.1 (overleaf), with the discounted rates for 2011–12 shown in the middle column.

Typically, you will be retired when you set up an account-based pension, but you are eligible to set one up once you reach age 65 even if you are still working, as at age 65 you have met a condition of release. Otherwise, most recipients of an account-based pension will be aged 55 to 64 and retired.

Once you start drawing an account-based pension, you can stop the pension and put your super back into accumulation mode if you want or need to. This may occur if you want to go back to work or not draw a pension for some reason or another. It is uncommon to do this, because you are usually better continuing to take the account-based pension and re-contributing the income back into super if you don't need it because of the tax benefits afforded to the pension structure (see below for more on this re-contribution strategy).

Account-based pensions are free of capital gains tax and earnings tax. And for over-60s the income drawn from an account-based pension is also free of income tax. If you are aged under 60 and over 55, your income will be taxed at your normal marginal tax rate, less a 15 per cent rebate (see chapter 9 for a discussion of how this works). Any non-taxable portion of your income stream will be free of tax too, so many people under the age of 60 also pay no tax. Many people delay retirement to age 60 because of the tax-free status of super for 60 years olds.

Table 10.1: minimum discounted and normal factors for an account-based pension

Age	Minimum annual factors (discounted — 2011–12) %	Minimum annual factors (normal) %
Under 65	3.00	4
65–74	3.75	5
75–79	4.50	6
80–84	5.25	7
85–89	6.75	9
90–94	8.25	11
95 and over	10.50	14

Source: <www.samhenderson.com.au>.

Re-contribution strategy

For those aged less than 60 and retired, a common strategy is to cash out the tax-free component from the taxable portion of your super (up to $165 000 in 2011–12 year), as well as some of the non-taxable component and re-contribute the lump sum into the super fund as a non-concessional contribution (up to $450 000) to increase your non-taxable component, to reduce or eliminate the amount of tax payable. This is called the re-contribution strategy. You should get advice on how to go about this, but it can save you thousands in income tax if you are under 60, and it will also save your non-dependent beneficiaries from paying the tax on your super benefits when you die. For this reason, it can also be used effectively for those aged 60 to 65 to increase the non-taxable component of their super, and thus reduce the effects of the death tax. Those who have reached 65 can also use this strategy, but they need to meet the work test rules (40 hours' work in any 30-day consecutive period) and they are restricted on the amount of non-concessional contributions they can make (that is, $150 000 non-concessional limit—see chapter 1 for details).

Let's look at an example. If your individual member balance is $750 000, made up of $300 000 (40 per cent of total) non-taxable and $450 000 (60 per cent of total) of taxable components, then in order to withdraw the first $165 000 of the taxable portion (which is actually tax-free and indexed up over time), you must withdraw it in proportion to your non-taxable component. Your taxable component is 40 per cent of your total balance and the non-taxable portion is 60 per cent, so in order to make a withdrawal of $165 000 from the taxable portion, you need to withdraw an equivalent portion from your non-taxable component. The $165 000 represents 36.66 per cent of your taxable component, so you need to withdraw 36.66 per cent of your non-taxable component of $300 000 at the same time—that would be $110 000. In total, you withdraw $275 000 from your fund and re-contribute it to the fund as a non-concessional contribution (it is below the $450 000 three-year averaging provision, but you will need to make sure you don't exceed your contribution caps over the three years if you have previously made contributions). The super balance remains the same, but the non-taxable proportion has increased from 38 per cent to 62 per cent of the total balance in the account. Table 10.2 (overleaf) shows how this works.

Table 10.2: the effect of a re-contribution strategy on a member's super balance

Component	Before strategy	After strategy
Taxable	$450 000 (60%)	$285 000 (38%)
Non-taxable	$300 000 (40%)	$465 000 (62%)
Total in fund	**$750 000**	**$750 000**
Withdrawal amount	**$275 000**	

The result is more of a benefit to non-dependent beneficiaries because the 15 per cent tax rebate afforded to under-60s would negate any tax payable under this situation (see the case study on p. 167). Surprisingly, most people don't pay tax under the age of 60 if they draw an account-based pension unless they earn other income. For this reason, I often recommend that clients don't wait until they are 60 to retire. Naturally, the longer you work and the more you contribute to super, the better off you will be, particularly if you have enough money to meet your lifestyle objectives.

What if one partner has a pension and the other is in accumulation mode?

Often one partner in an SMSF retires earlier than the other, and you may have part of your total fund in pension mode and another part in accumulation mode. There are ways to manage this from a paperwork perspective.

You will need to get an annual actuarial certificate, which may cost around $150 to $400, to determine who owns what percentage of assets in the fund as part of their pension. Alternatively, you can segregate the assets from the commencement of the pension and reduce the need for an actuarial certificate to once every three years.

Segregating the assets is reasonably easy if the assets are held in cash or certain types of shares but, more often than not, the assets of an SMSF are pooled for investment purposes so it may be deemed that each member owns a certain percentage and so an actuarial certificate may be required to determine whose assets are whose and by what percentage. In this case, the actuarial certificate will be an annual requirement since the assets are not segregated, but if assets are segregated you can span it out to every three years. This is also the case with a transition to retirement pension, where part of the pension is in accumulation mode and part in pension mode.

Case study: account-based pension for a member under age 60 (age 55 to 59)

Richard and Jane have $1 200 000 in their super fund. Richard retires at age 55 and Jane is 53 and still working. Richard has $750 000 in his member balance, of which $300 000 is non-taxable and $450 000 is taxable. Richard is going to draw his minimum pension of 4 per cent as Jane is still working and he doesn't really need the income. He plans to re-contribute the income into Jane's member balance as a non-concessional contribution to boost her balance before she retires in a few years.

Richard's tax situation would look like this:

Member balance at 1 July	$750 000
Minimum 4 per cent of account balance	$30 000
Taxable (60 per cent of balance/income)	$18 000
Non-taxable (40 per cent of balance/income)	$12 000
Tax on taxable portion	$1980
15 per cent rebate of taxable portion (up to)	$2700
Actual tax payable (owing to rebate)	$0

Assuming Richard has no other income, his $30 000 income will be tax free once his 15 per cent rebate has been taken into account. This is the case for many people under the age 60, despite the blanket tax-free status for over-60s. The re-contribution strategy would really be of benefit only to his non-dependants to reduce tax on his death or to boost Jane's super balance (through a non-concessional contribution) and even up the balances, which could reduce tax for Jane's pension or her beneficiaries.

Richard's investments in his pension account in the fund would also be free from earnings tax. That means he will be able to claim back 100 per cent of any franking credits he receives if he owns shares in his SMSF, increasing his income significantly. He would also be investing free of capital gains tax, which is another important attribute of account-based pensions.

Case study: account-based pension for a member age 60 and above

Richard's situation would be no different once he reaches age 60, except that he wouldn't bother with the 15 per cent tax rebate on the taxable portion of his $30 000 income, because his income would simply be tax-free. His investment income and capital gains tax in his pension account would be nil.

How to set up your account-based pension

When you want to set up an account-based pension, speak to your adviser or SMSF administrator or accountant and they will use a series of documents and processes that I call our pension pack. A pension pack is simply what I use for my clients and it is a series of questions, documents and processes detailing the following aspects of your intention to move to pension phase:

- What type of pension do you want? (TRIS or account-based?)

- When do you want to commence it?

- How much do you want to draw? Just the minimum or specified amount?

- How often do you want to receive your pension? (You must take it at least annually, but usually people take payments every month.)

- What is the name and address of the member/trustee drawing the pension?

- What are the bank account details of the recipient (can be a joint account)?

- Have all trustees been notified that the member will be starting a pension?

- What is the name of the reversionary beneficiary?

It will also have a retirement declaration and other minutes to detail conditions of release.

Once the above specifications have been detailed a Pension Agreement is constructed into a single document that also deals with aspects of the pension, such as variations, ceasing the pension and what happens in the event of death. As an SMSF trustee, this is a prudent and well-documented approach that would be compliant in the eyes of the tax office in the event of an audit. It may also be good to have a declaration of retirement attached to this document to confirm the new pensioner has satisfied a condition of release.

What happens to my transition to retirement income stream (TRIS) at retirement?

You can leave your TRIS in place if you are happy with the income levels that you are drawing, as you do not have to make too many changes. Certain restrictions will be lifted, such as the restriction under a TRIS that you cannot make lump sum withdrawals (commutations) above 10 per cent of the account value. Your income stream will then be deemed to be an account-based pension instead of a TRIS. You can even leave your accumulation portion in place until age 65. I recommend people do this in case they want to do some part-time work or consulting, or want to make some more contributions to super for any reason, such as in the event of an asset sale outside super and moving the proceeds into the tax-free super environment.

The Age Pension

Another consideration once you are over the age of 65 (possibly earlier for some women) is the government Age Pension, administered by Centrelink. To check if you are eligible for an Age Pension, two tests are applied to your financial situation: the assets test and the income test. Whichever one produces the lower Age Pension for you is the one they apply to you.

Each half-year in March and September the income and assets test are indexed to reflect changes in average earnings (AWOTE—average weekly ordinary time earnings). In September 2011, for example, the assets test upper limit for a home-owning couple was $1 018 000, at which point you would not be eligible to receive any Age Pension. Visit the Centrelink website <www.centrelink.gov.au> for regular updates and full details of the means test and levels of pension payments, or speak to a Centrelink financial information service officer (FISO) before you reach your Age Pension age so you know where you stand and what might be available to you.

Effectively you can be a millionaire and receive some part-pension from Centrelink, which will also qualify you to receive the low income pension card (different from the state-based Seniors Card and the Commonwealth Seniors Health Card) for discounts on utilities and other services worth more than about $2000 to $3000 a year. So it's worth trying to get at least something from Centrelink.

Commonwealth Seniors Health Card

Another benefit for seniors is the Commonwealth Seniors Health Card. You are eligible if you are over Age Pension age and earning less than $80 000 per year as a couple or less than $50 000 a year as a single. This card will allow you to obtain cheap pharmaceuticals and in recent budgets it has also attracted some cash rebates to cardholders. Again, Centrelink will assist here, so visit their website or call 13 23 00 to book an appointment.

Seniors Cards

State-based Seniors Cards are also available to people over age 60 and working less than 20 hours a week (a different definition to retirement so be careful). This card provides benefits such as cheap travel and a host of other discounts on a multitude of products and services. Visit the Seniors Card website at <www.seniorscard.com.au> for more information and it will direct you to information for your state.

Key points

¤   You can go back to work after you retire if you want to.

¤   You can continue to contribute to super after you retire if you are under age 65.

¤   If you want to contribute to super after age 65, you have to work at least 40 hours in any 30-day consecutive period in the financial year in which you want to make contributions.

◻ An account-based pension is the main form of SMSF income stream once you retire.

◻ An account-based pension is very flexible.

◻ Once an account-based pension has been commenced, you can stop it if you like and revert to accumulation mode in your super fund.

◻ You must take a minimum amount each year but there is no maximum withdrawal.

◻ You can make lump sum withdrawals.

◻ You can receive payments according to a schedule you set, provided you take at least one payment a year.

◻ No capital gains tax or earnings tax is payable on income streams or lump sums paid from a super pension account, and even under age 60 most people don't pay tax if they have no other income. Account-based pensions and lump sums are free of income tax for over-60s.

◻ You can use a re-contribution strategy to reduce tax if you are aged less than 60 if you are paying a little tax. It may also be useful for reducing the tax on super benefits for non-dependent beneficiaries.

◻ If you are of Age Pension age, check your eligibility for payments and benefits with Centrelink, and talk to a financial information service officer (FISO).

CHAPTER 11

Estate planning

No one wants to die. Even people who want to go to heaven don't want to die to get there. And yet death is the destination we all share. No one has ever escaped it. And that is as it should be, because Death is very likely the single best invention of Life. It is Life's change agent. It clears out the old to make way for the new. Right now the new is you, but someday not too long from now, you will gradually become the old and be cleared away. Sorry to be so dramatic, but it is quite true.

Steve Jobs, Commencement address at Stanford University,
12 June 2005

One of the key features of an SMSF is the benefits it offers for estate planning. Not only do you have supreme control over your investments, but you also have similar influence over the way your superannuation assets pass to beneficiaries. For example, superannuation dependants can receive a deceased person's tax-free account-based pension without having to cash out the assets from the super system. This means that pensions can remain free of income tax, earnings tax and capital gains tax long after you have left this world, funding your dependants with much-needed income and access to capital.

Assets inside your SMSF can also pass immediately to dependants within the fund, skipping the whole probate process or avoiding challenges to your will by disgruntled family members. The settling of wills can take months, if not years if challenges slow down the process, and financially dependent beneficiaries can suffer, despite the best intentions of the deceased. A binding nomination form for beneficiaries in an SMSF can ensure the assets pass directly to the dependants, reducing timing risk for the distribution of assets and income. Non-dependants are excluded from the binding nomination, but the definition of dependants under superannuation law is different from that under tax law (see table 11.1 on p. 177).

While many people establish SMSFs with the intention of improving their estate planning, the subject of estate planning is poorly understood, not only by member/trustees but also by the legal community. It is possible, for instance, for partners in a couple to obtain mirror wills for a few hundred dollars, but it is unlikely to adequately deal with the management of your SMSF, and don't even think about a $25 Will Kit if you have an SMSF. It's worth forking out some of your hard-earned cash for a good estate plan, given your choice of an SMSF and given the fact that you have spent the time and money to increase your own control over your assets.

Your estate plan is your passing gift to your beneficiaries who will be busy looking after you in the event of illness or disability or mourning your passing. Do not burden them with unnecessary administrative or financial distress by not having a bullet-proof estate plan.

What assets can be covered by your will?

Will assets are assets dealt with by your will in the event of your death. However, many common assets that you would expect to be dealt with under your will actually fall outside its control. For example, if your family home is owned in joint names, your half is not dealt with by your will. In fact, your half will pass immediately and automatically to the surviving joint owner and skip the will process altogether. This is a good risk management technique, as wills are subject to challenges by a host of people and challenges can slow down the distribution of assets in a time of need for beneficiaries.

If you are in a de facto relationship or second marriage and you want to pass your half of a jointly owned asset (like your house) to someone other than the joint owner, you can apply to have the asset held as tenants in common without the handover of the asset triggering capital gains tax or stamp duty. In the case of a second marriage, you may have children from a first marriage that you would like to receive your half of the property. In this case, you could change the ownership status for the asset to tenants in common (50/50 share) and your half could be dealt with under your will and distributed to your children. (See chapter 13 in *Financial Planning DIY Guide* for more information about estate planning for individuals.)

Tip

Some of your largest assets might not actually be among the assets covered by your will, for example, a home or other jointly held assets, or your superannuation balance, because superannuation is in fact held in a trust.

Your SMSF assets can also fall outside of your will. As an SMSF member/trustee, it's important that you understand what assets fall within the realm of superannuation law. Your SMSF is a trust and the distribution of trust assets therefore falls outside of your will. That being said, if no instruction is given, your SMSF funds will be dealt with by the executor of your will, and the assets would be distributed under the normal instructions contained in your will.

What is a binding nomination of beneficiaries?

An important function of your super fund is to provide death benefits to beneficiaries when you pass away. Your SMSF balance (or pensions to dependants) can be left to beneficiaries through your will or directly to beneficiaries by nominating specific dependants in a binding nomination of beneficiaries. You can only nominate dependants as defined under superannuation law, such as a spouse (husband, wife, same sex or de facto), children or any other financial dependants or interdependants.

In every super fund you can fill in a form, known as a *Nomination of beneficiaries* form, to say who you want to receive your super in the event of your death, and your fund must take your wishes into account when it pays out your super benefits after your death. However, they don't *have* to follow your instructions. To ensure the trustees of the fund do exactly what you want, you need to fill in a *Binding nomination of beneficiaries* form. Both kinds of nomination operate in all super funds, including SMSFs. Binding nominations have some special rules attached to them, but having one in place makes a lot of sense.

A superannuation binding death nomination is an instruction given to the surviving member/trustees of your SMSF to distribute your superannuation assets to your chosen beneficiaries. If a binding death nomination has not been made or has expired, the trustees can distribute the death benefits at their discretion, and there have been cases where they have distributed the funds to themselves. Trustees do not have any discretion if the nomination is binding, and assets must be distributed to nominees at the earliest convenience.

To make a valid and effective binding death nomination you must:

¤ make sure your trust deed allows for a binding nomination (if not, update your trust deed)

¤ nominate whether it is a binding or discretionary nomination

¤ specify the name of your fund

¤ specify the name(s) of the beneficiaries and provide their contact details, their relationship to you and the percentage of your super you want them to get.

You may only nominate superannuation dependants in binding or discretionary nominations, so it's important to understand who is an eligible dependant under super rules because superannuation law differs slightly from the tax laws, with some potentially taxing consequences.

The differences between dependants under the SIS Act versus tax law are shown in table 11.1.

Table 11.1: definition of dependants under super versus tax law

Person	Super law	Tax law
Spouse	Yes	Yes
Same-sex spouse	Yes	Yes
Child (under 18)	Yes	Yes
Child (over 18)	Yes	No
Financial interdependence	Yes	Yes

The consequences of these rules is that, while under superannuation law you can choose who will get your assets, you cannot control how those assets will be taxed in the hands of the beneficiaries. For example, you can choose to distribute half of your superannuation to an adult child (over 18 and financially independent), but the tax office will slug them with 16.5 per cent tax on your taxable component. If you are over age 60, retired and suffering from a terminal illness, you can cash out your super tax-free and simply give it to an adult child free of tax as a gift (gifting rules only affect those on the Age Pension, talk to Centrelink or visit their website for more details).

> **Tip**
> Make sure your binding death nomination is updated every three years or when there is a change in your circumstances, such as marriage or divorce, the birth of a child or the death of a spouse.

It is possible to construct a mechanism to distribute assets from your super fund into a tax-effective trust on your death to benefit non-dependants under super law (and dependants). This trust is called a testamentary trust, or a will trust, and it is established on death to hold assets and distribute income to beneficiaries for tax-effectiveness and asset protection. See the section on page 181 for more information on testamentary trusts.

Updating and ensuring the validity of a binding nomination of beneficiaries

A binding nomination of beneficiaries expires after three years, although there have been many calls to government to change this law to allow for perpetual nominations. In the absence of legal changes, it is therefore advisable that you make a diary note to update your nomination every three years to ensure your estate planning objectives are fulfilled. Many retail and industry funds send reminder notices when nominations expire, but since you are your own trustee, you need to ensure you have a reminder or regularly check the expiration date.

To ensure your nomination of beneficiaries is valid, legal and binding, it must also be in writing, and signed and dated by the member and two independent witnesses who are aged over 18 and not beneficiaries. This is similar to a will. Your nomination must also contain a declaration signed, and dated, by the witnesses, stating that the notice was signed by the member in their presence. Without these strict criteria being satisfied the death benefit nominations will not be binding upon the trustees.

With around 50 per cent of marriages ending in divorce, you can imagine the possible conflicts of interest that may arise in the event of superannuation asset distribution. A binding nomination helps to remove any uncertainty around the issue, so if you have an existing nomination, make sure that it is up to date, valid and reflects your objectives — right now! And if it is not a binding nomination, change it to a binding nomination right now. So, too, if your circumstances change, such as marriage, divorce, death of dependants, children reaching 18 or moving out of home, you should update your binding nomination of beneficiaries as soon as possible.

Wills

While the objective of this chapter is to educate you on the estate planning features, benefits and pitfalls of SMSFs, I'll give you a quick overview of wills and testamentary trusts as this information provides an important background to the operations and importance of estate planning for you. There are some considerations for all situations affecting your SMSF money that you may want to think about when preparing your will.

A will is a legal document that details your intentions for the distribution of your assets in the event of your death. More than 40 per cent of Australians die intestate (without a will) so your first objective should be to construct a legally valid will and ensure it continues to meet your objectives over time and in the face of changing family dynamics, such as divorce, marriage, additional children and the death of beneficiaries or executors. Dying intestate may create significant problems for beneficiaries as your intentions cannot be fulfilled. The state will make decisions on what happens to your estate, which can delay the distribution of assets for a long time and disadvantage those in need.

The state governments deal with estates and so the laws differ from state to state. If you have moved recently, make sure your will is appropriate for your current state. A will may cost around $500 to more than $3000 depending on the complexity of your situation. Simple mirror wills (one each), 'Mum leaves it all to Dad and Dad leaves it all to Mum', may cost between $500 and $900 if done by a local solicitor, but if you have an SMSF, you may want to discuss some more tailored options.

A valid will must be:

¤ in writing

¤ signed by the will-maker (who may not be under duress or of unsound mind)

¤ signed by two independent witnesses who are:

  ■ over age 18

  ■ not a beneficiary

  ■ physically present for witnessing your signature.

A variation of any of the conditions above can give rise to a challenge to the will and the estate assets. Wills can also be invalidated by marriage and divorce, and can be challenged by spouses, ex-spouses, children, stepchildren, siblings or anyone considered financially dependent or having an interdependent relationship, such as same-sex partnerships. To minimise the chance of a challenge or to successfully defend a challenge, it is best to mention all parties in a will, even if you don't want to give them anything. You could also give them a token gift to recognise them so they aren't left out entirely.

Who are the parties to a will?

The main parties to a will and their roles are:

- *Testator or testatrix (female)* — the will-maker and the original owner of the estate (the deceased).

- *Executor* — the person or entity appointed under the will to administer the estate of the testator. The executor is responsible for the identification, administration and distribution of the assets, according to the law.

- *Beneficiary* — a person or entity who receives assets or benefits from the distribution of the estate on the death of the testator.

- *Administrator* — in the event that a person dies without appointing an executor, an administrator is appointed to administer the estate to act as an executor. In the case of someone dying intestate, the prospective administrator will have to apply for a Grant of Letter of Administration to provide them with the requisite power to act for the estate.

Probate — the administration of estate

Probate is simply a process of establishing that a valid will exists and that the executor has the authority to act on behalf of the estate. It is an application to the Supreme Court in your state, and the legal document that you apply for is called a Grant of Probate.

The court registers the will and verifies its validity before granting probate. Once granted, the executor can gain access to bank accounts and set about assembling the deceased's assets and liabilities, administering them and then distributing the remaining assets of the estate to beneficiaries. Administration includes preparing tax returns, finding bank accounts, assembling assets, buying or selling assets, and paying bills. Depending on the state of the will, and complexity of the instructions and assets, the probate process may take anything from a couple of months to a couple of years.

For example, if the will allows for cash to be distributed to a number of beneficiaries then a property may have to be sold before there is any cash available to distribute. The land titles office may also be involved in the transfer of a property to a beneficiary if the will allowed for a particular property to be passed to a specific beneficiary.

The role of the executor is an important one and it carries with it a great legal responsibility to act in the best interests of beneficiaries and the testator. Most people appoint their spouse or children as their executor, but the role can be taken by a trusted adviser or even a professional organisation that administers estates (although that is not recommended). The role is time consuming and it can require some considerable effort, including the assistance of a solicitor, which can be costly. The estate pays costs of the administration and advice, as well as the immediate costs of the funeral arrangements. The job can be quite challenging, especially if being carried out by a member of a grieving family, so be prepared to do some work if someone appoints you as an executor.

Testamentary trusts

A testamentary trust, also known as a will trust, can be established on the death of a person to protect the deceased's assets. One of the key reasons to establish a testamentary trust is to distribute tax-effective income to minors, as minors will not pay the highest marginal tax rate on the income as they would otherwise do. Income paid to minors through a testamentary trust is taxed under the normal marginal tax rates for adults, which includes a tax-free threshold (currently $6000).

As an SMSF member/trustee, it may be worth leaving some of your non-super estate to grandchildren for education or investment purposes to help out them out in the future. While grandchildren would not be considered to be financial dependants, a testamentary trust allows you to pass on some tax-effective assets to them which would not be afforded to them if their parents bought assets in their name. They would then be liable for 45 per cent tax on all earnings as well as capital gains tax.

Another great reason for establishing a testamentary trust is to protect the assets from adversarial former spouses or de factos of beneficiaries. The assets in a testamentary trust can be controlled by the intended beneficiaries and be accessible for the use of beneficiaries, but the assets can be protected from former spouses or de factos in the event of dispute or family breakdown. This is particularly effective when a parent, for example, doesn't like the de facto partner of an adult child and thinks that the relationship will not last. In the event of a relationship breakdown and after the parent has died, the parent's assets can be held in trust for the child and the de facto partner will have no right to the assets held in the trust.

In this example, if the assets were passed directly to the adult child on the parent's death and, say, the child paid down the mortgage on a jointly owned property with the de facto, the de facto would have a good argument to claim half of the value of the property in the event of a relationship breakdown. This would be strongly against the wishes of the deceased parent and the parent's assets would be lost to an adversary of the family. The testamentary trust is designed to protect the family's assets.

> **Tip**
>
> Testamentary trusts are great for distributing income to minors and protecting assets from the partners of adult children in the event of their relationship breakdown, including marriage, de facto or same-sex couples — they are all treated in the same way.

A testamentary trust can also be established to look after disabled children or partners (a disability trust) or other beneficiaries who cannot look after themselves. This is also a good method of looking after adults who are not capable of managing money, such as drug addicts, alcoholics or other adults who display forms of addiction combined with poor money management skills. The estate can, for example, be instructed to pay rent and repay an account at a supermarket rather than paying cash to someone who might misuse it.

Power of attorney

A power of attorney is a document that allows someone to act on your behalf subject to any conditions contained within the document. This is particularly handy if you are unable to attend to an important matter because of incapacity, travel (inability to attend) or disability.

The person granting the power of attorney to another person is called the donor and the person who is the grantee is called the attorney. A power of attorney is revoked on death, bankruptcy or insolvency or at time that is set for expiry. There are two types of powers of attorney:

¤   general power of attorney

¤   enduring power of attorney.

A general power of attorney allows a person to act on the donor's behalf to sign documents, attend meetings, and basically act as the donor except in financial (no bank account operations or access to money), lifestyle or medical situations. The general power of attorney ceases to apply if the donor becomes of unsound mind.

An enduring power of attorney allows the attorney to make financial decisions and will continue if the donor becomes of unsound mind. In fact, this is often the intention of an enduring power of attorney and it ideal for elderly people with Alzheimer's disease or who are incapacitated because of physical or mental illness. However, if they already have the disease (and so are of unsound mind) it is too late to sign an enduring power of attorney, as they will not have legal capacity. So it's best to have all this documentation in place as early in life as possible and update it regularly as life changes.

In the event that an enduring power of attorney has not been set up and a person becomes of unsound mind, then an administrator or guardian may need to be appointed through a state government agency or Supreme Court. This is best addressed by having a power of attorney drawn up as early as possible so that people who know you make decisions about your welfare in a speedy and well-informed manner.

For SMSF members/trustees, an enduring power of attorney or the appointment of a legal personal representative can be given to other SMSF members or trusted external parties to make investment and administrative decisions for a member moving overseas. You can download the ruling from the ATO that deals with this matter by going to <www.ato.gov.au>, clicking on 'legal database' and searching for SMSFR 2010/2. This ruling deals specifically with SMSFs and the operation of powers of attorney for replacing a trustee member to manage the fund.

Generally, you need to be a resident to establish and maintain your SMSF, but by giving another member/trustee an enduring power of attorney, you may be excused if you move overseas for more than two years. The ruling details the operation of how a member is to be replaced. A power of attorney:

> can be used by a trustee, or a director of the corporate trustee, of a SMSF to retain the fund's 'central management and control' in Australia when the trustee is overseas for an extended period

> can be used by a trustee, or a director of the corporate trustee, of a SMSF to ensure that the fund retains its status as a SMSF in situations where a trustee no longer wants to perform their duties as trustee or director of the corporate trustee

> operates independently of, and is not restricted by, any exclusions contained in state or territory power of attorney legislation against conferring trustee duties and powers via a power of attorney

> does not require that a member be replaced as a trustee, or a director of the corporate trustee, by a legal personal representative on a one-for-one basis

> allows a member to appoint a legal personal representative as an 'alternate director' of the corporate trustee.

The ruling also provides a variety of examples that you can apply to your own circumstances. These include:

> transferring your employment to an overseas company for an indefinite period of time

> travelling overseas and executing an enduring power of attorney in favour of another member

> nearing retirement and wanting to transfer the responsibilities of being a trustee of the SMSF.

Among the duties and scope of your normal powers of attorney you can include the requirement that would enable your attorney to cash out your super in the event of your illness, disability or incapacity. This helps to avoid the death tax and capital gains tax imposed on non-dependant beneficiaries for super and super pensions.

Remember I discussed the 'death tax', whereby a non-dependant beneficiary, such as a financially independent adult child, pays tax on the taxable portion of your superannuation distributed by an estate? This can be avoided if a member is dying slowly, because they can cash out their super tax-free if they are over 60 and have met a condition of release.

Many powers of attorney people set up don't adequately deal with superannuation. It's important that if you do receive the advice of a solicitor that you instruct them to address the issue of superannuation and the ability for attorneys to manage superannuation in the event of illness, disability or imminent death. Powers of attorney for SMSFs can also address the management of a fund in the event of a trustee moving overseas for more than two years.

Key points

¤ Member/trustees of SMSFs must understand the essentials of estate planning.

¤ Make sure you understand what assets are dealt with in your will, which ones skip the will process and what happens to your super when you die.

¤ By having a correct and comprehensive set of documentation in place, your intentions for the distribution of your assets and superannuation can be fulfilled in the most tax-effective form for beneficiaries.

¤ Dependants receive your super or pension tax-free.

¤ The death tax is a 16.5 per cent tax on the taxable portion of your super fund when it is paid to non-dependants. The non-taxable portion remains tax-free for both dependants and non-dependants.

¤ Make sure each member/trustee of the SMSF has a valid and up-to-date binding nomination of beneficiaries in place, and ensure it is updated every three years.

¤ Assets paid out through a binding nomination of beneficiaries will skip the will and probate process, and are transferred directly to the beneficiary (not into the beneficiary's super but to them personally—only reversionary beneficiaries, such as a surviving spouse or financially dependent child, can receive a pension; check your trust deed for these details and permission for reversionary beneficiaries).

¤   A valid and up-to-date will ensures your assets are distributed to the right people when you die.

¤   Marriage and divorce nullify existing wills, so keep wills up to date.

¤   Testamentary trusts help distribute non-super income to minors tax-effectively.

¤   Enduring powers of attorney can assist SMSF trustees to manage their funds effectively if they are incapacitated or overseas.

¤   Essentially, everyone should have an enduring power of attorney, whether they have an SMSF or not.

CHAPTER 12

10 strategies to reduce your tax and boost your super

In real life, strategy is actually very straightforward. You pick a general direction and implement like hell.

Jack Welch, former CEO General Electric (1981–2001),
net worth $720 million

This chapter summarises the key strategies that an SMSF expert adviser might recommend to help you reduce your tax and boost your super. While many of these have already been used as examples throughout the book, this chapter groups them together and shows how they work through case studies. These ten strategies should be reviewed whenever you reach a benchmark age, such as 50, 55, 60, 65 or 75, when a significant financial event occurs, such as the sale of an asset or business, or an inheritance or windfall, or as an integral part of your retirement planning.

Unfortunately, many people miss out on the supreme benefits of superannuation strategies because they don't understand the system, but it's not as difficult as some people claim. Following these ten strategies can make a huge difference to your retirement savings, adding hundreds of thousands of dollars to the end result, so make sure you read this chapter carefully.

Don't discount this chapter if you are under age 50, as there are many strategies that can be used in your 30s and 40s. At age 39, I have already used salary sacrifice, the small business capital gains tax (CGT) concession, CGT reduction strategy, super splitting and gearing into shares and property, so don't think superannuation is just for the over-50s. The earlier you start in super, the better off you will be. So many times I hear clients say that they wished they had known how to use the benefits of an SMSF earlier. Don't delay implementing these strategies — do it now!

Strategy 1: salary sacrifice to reduce income tax and boost your super

One of the first strategies you should implement is salary sacrifice. In this strategy, you put a portion of your before-tax salary into your super fund as a concessional contribution instead of taking it as part of your monthly pay. Your salary sacrifice contributions will be taxed at 15 per cent by the super fund and not in the hands of your employer. The money is sacrificed because you can't touch it until you meet of condition of release. The idea is that you put more than your superannuation guarantee amount of 9 per cent a year into super to boost your balance and you get the added benefit of saving tax.

Given that most full-time workers earn more than $37 000 a year, they will pay more than 15 per cent tax on their earnings. By putting money into your superannuation and paying the 15 per cent contributions tax, you will be better off by up to 66 per cent if you are highest on the marginal tax rate of 45 per cent. If you are paying 30 per cent tax (income greater than $37 000 per year), you will be better off by 50 per cent. So salary sacrifice makes sense. (Note that tax brackets will change over time, so the threshold where 30 per cent begins will change over time.) Often increasing your salary sacrifice doesn't greatly affect your take-home pay, owing to the tax savings, but that will depend upon the level at which you salary sacrifice.

It's important that you understand your cash flow properly so you can accurately work out how much salary sacrifice you can afford. If you do get it wrong, you can change the amount fairly easily (ask your employer about how often you can change), so don't worry too much as it may require some playing around to find the perfect amount to put away each month. If you work for someone, have a chat to the payroll department or person to make sure they are comfortable with how to make your contributions and make sure that you have a choice of fund and they have your SMSF details. Some employers don't have a choice of fund and you may have to salary sacrifice into a fund stipulated in your employment contract; however, you may be able to sweep that money out regularly and transfer it into your SMSF. If this is not possible, then you may have to wait to retirement or resignation to roll your super over but that is unlikely unless you have defined benefit super. Even if you have defined benefit super, you will have a member portion in your super that should be available for rolling into your SMSF.

Case study: salary sacrifice

Judy, aged 52, is earning $75 000 a year and is in the 30 per cent tax bracket for all income earned over $37 000 and below $80 000 for the 2012 financial year. Her cost of living, when apportioned with her partner, is around $30 000 after tax. On an income of $75 000, she would pay $17 150 in tax, leaving her with $57 850 in take-home pay. If Judy needs only $30 000 after tax, she should salary sacrifice some of her pay into super to reduce her income tax bill and boost her super. Currently, Judy's employer puts in 9 per cent super guarantee amount of $6750 (9 per cent × $75 000), but she is not salary sacrificing anything at present.

Most people simply spend their excess salary, although some do save a portion or put it into mortgage repayments or investments. We will assume Judy usually spends the excess on travel and other discretionary items.

I would recommend Judy salary sacrifices $38 000 a year into her super fund in addition to her employer's contribution of 9 per cent of her salary (adjusted to $37 000 from $75 000). Legally, your employer only has to pay your super guarantee on your post-salary sacrifice income so your 9 per cent superannuation guarantee amount may fall if your employer is aware of this—many aren't. As Judy is over age 50 and has less than $500 000 in her super fund, she is eligible to salary sacrifice up to $50 000 a year into her super. She would also be able to put in up to $150 000 as a non-concessional contribution if she had the money (or up to $450 000 under the three-year averaging provision).

(cont'd)

Case study: salary sacrifice *(cont'd)*

If Judy contributes $38 000 to her super by salary sacrifice, she will save a total annual tax amount of $8153 and be around $520 000 better off at age 65 when she retires with a little under $1 000 000 in her super. While many people know how to salary sacrifice, many don't quantify it or implement a strategy by taking action — there is a big difference between knowing and doing. Another big issue with salary sacrifice is that some people have stopped doing it because investment markets have been volatile, but this is not a good reason to stop salary sacrificing. Change your investment strategy to more cash and fixed interest, or benefit from the rebound by investing when shares are cheaper, but do not forgo the tax benefits of salary sacrifice.

How Judy's salary sacrifice will work is shown in table 12.1.

Table 12.1: Judy's salary sacrifice

	Current strategy (do nothing)	Recommended ($38 000 salary sacrifice)
Income	$75 000	$37 000
Income tax	$17 125	$3 985
Net income	$57 875	$33 015
Employer SG (%)	9%	9%
Employer SG $	$6 750	$3 330
Household expenses	$30 000	$30 000
Salary sacrifice	$0	$38 000
Contributions tax at 15%	$0	$5 700
Total contributions tax	$1 013	$6 000
Total tax paid	$18 138	$9 985
Total tax savings	$0	$8 153
Super balance at age 52	$200 000	$200 000
Super balance at age 65	$478 758.07	$999 395.77
Value of strategy		**$520 637.70**

Note: Assumes salary remains unchanged and growth rate of funds is 5 per cent per year.

The effect of Judy's salary sacrifice on her super balance is shown in table 12.2.

Table 12.2: benefits of salary sacrifice

Age	Super balance* (do nothing)	Super balance* (salary sacrificing)
52	$200 000.00	$200 000.00
53	$215 737.00	$245 130.50
54	$232 261.00	$292 517.53
55	$249 612.00	$342 273.90
56	$267 830.00	$394 518.10
57	$286 959.00	$449 374.50
58	$307 045.00	$506 973.73
59	$328 134.00	$567 452.91
61	$373 530.00	$697 634.36
62	$397 944.00	$767 646.58
63	$423 579.00	$841 159.41
64	$450 495.00	$918 347.88
65	$478 758.07	$999 395.77
Value of strategy		**$520 637.70**

Note: Assumes salary remains unchanged and growth rate of funds is 5 per cent per year.

*All figures rounded to whole numbers.

> **Tip**
>
> Salary sacrifice will save you income tax and boost your retirement savings.

Strategy 2: co-contributions — it's money for nothing!

If you earn less than $31 920 and you make a non-concessional super-annuation contribution to super of $1000, the government will give you an extra $1000 in your super fund when you complete your personal tax return. That's a 100 per cent return on your money — guaranteed! The co-contribution is perfect for part-time workers, including university students with part-time jobs, apprentices and working mums. If you don't have $1000 spare, then you can contribute less and still receive a bonus based on the amount contributed. For example, if you earn less than $31 920 and contribute $200, your super will get a $200 payment from the government.

The amount due to you will reduce by 3.333 cents for every dollar you earn over $31 920 up to a maximum of $61 920, when you will no longer be eligible for a bonus. In late 2011, the co-contribution amounts were based on the calculations shown in table 12.3.

Table 12.3: how co-contributions are calculated, 2009–12

Time frame	Lower income threshold	Higher income threshold	What will I receive for every $1 of eligible personal super contributions?	What is my maximum entitlement?
From 1 July 2009 until 30 June 2012	$31 920	$61 920	$1, up to your maximum entitlement	Your maximum entitlement is $1000 if you earn less than $31 920.

Note: This reduces by 3.333 cents for every dollar your total income, less allowable business deductions, exceeds $31 920, up to $61 920.

If you earn more than $31 920 and less than $61 920 you will receive a partial bonus. For example, if you contribute $1000 and earn $50 000, you will receive around $400; if you earn around $59 000, you will receive around $100. It is proposed that the rate for the co-contribution will increase over time for the next few financial years.

Please note that while the above information is relevant until 30 June 2012, there have been some proposed changes in the Federal Government's mini-budget in November 2011. It is proposed that from 1 July 2012 the co-contribution will be reduced by 50 per cent from $1000 to $500. An additional bonus will be given to superannuants in the form of an up-to $500 rebate on superannuation contributions tax for those with taxable income under $37 000 per annum. This is similar to the co-contribution for low-income earners. The co-contribution will be wound back and the upper limit for eligibility will fall from $61 920 to $46 920.

A good strategy for parents to encourage young working-age children to contribute to superannuation is to match their co-contribution.

For example, suggest to your kids that if they put $500 into their super, you will match it with $500, and then they will receive the full co-contribution from the government of $1000. Strategies like these can help to build superannuation awareness for young people and start their retirement savings as early as possible.

Tip

The co-contribution is money for nothing and a guaranteed 100 to 150 per cent return on your money so there's no excuses for not making a non-concessional contribution if you earn less than $62 000 a year.

Strategy 3: small business CGT exemptions—pay no CGT on the sale of your business

If you have owned your business, possibly including the premises, for more than 15 years and its total value is less than $6 million, then you may reduce or eliminate capital gains tax on the sale of these assets. You can also put up to $1.2 million from their sale tax-free into super.

Four main exemptions are available to business owners who meet the right conditions. The right conditions are that your business must be classed as small, with a turnover of less than $2 million or net assets of less than $6 million. The small business assets must be active assets within the business, which can include goodwill, stock and even your premises. You also need to be what the tax office calls a significant individual, who has 20 per cent or more ownership of the business.

The four exemptions (described below) can be used simultaneously. These are:

¤   15-year exemption

¤   additional 50 per cent CGT discount (on top of regular 12-month ownership 50 per cent discount)

¤ $500 000 retirement exemption

¤   CGT rollover provision.

15-year exemption

If you have owned your business for 15 years or more, and you meet the small business conditions, you can sell your business free of capital gains tax.

Additional 50 per cent CGT discount

If you have owned your business for fewer than 15 years and you meet the conditions, you may receive a further 50 per cent discount in addition to the regular 50 per cent reduction you obtain for owning an asset for more than 12 months.

$500 000 retirement rollover

You may receive a one-time $500 000 CGT rollover. That means you can eliminate $500 000 of capital gain at any time in your life when you sell your business. If you are under age 55, you do have to roll the $500 000 over into your super fund.

CGT rollover provision

Under this provision you can defer all or part of the capital gains from a CGT tax event for two years or more, under two conditions:

¤   you purchase a replacement asset

¤   you improve an existing asset.

The beauty of these exemptions is that they can be used simultaneously. For example, if you don't meet the 15-year rule, you can still get a further 50 per cent CGT reduction, a $500 000 retirement exemption and the CGT rollover.

If you are in a position to sell a small business, it's a good idea to get advice, and also download the information booklet *Advanced Guide to Capital Gains Tax Concessions for Small Business* (NAT 3359) from the tax office website <www.ato.gov.au>. Make sure you speak to a specialist in this area and someone has worked through a few real-life examples, as the conditions and concessions can be quite complex.

> **Tip**
>
> If you own a small business (and business premises) and you plan to sell it, make sure you seek advice about how to reduce your capital gains tax.

Strategy 4: use a transition to retirement income stream to reduce tax and increase super

A transition to retirement income stream (TRIS) is a superannuation pension you can set up while you are still working. You can use the income stream from the TRIS to subsidise your work income while you increase your concessional contributions to super, paying just 15 per cent contributions tax up to $50 000 per year, instead of the 30, 37 or 45 per cent tax rate on your normal pay. It's like recycling your money to reduce your tax by drawing down on your super and salary sacrificing simultaneously. The government allows this because they want you to be at least partially self-funded in retirement.

In order to be eligible to commence a TRIS, you need to be aged over 55 and less than age 65. Once you reach age 65, you have met a normal condition of release and can commence a full account-based pension. If you have a TRIS, you can draw only between 4 per cent and 10 per cent of the account balance at 1 July (or set-up date) each year, and you cannot withdraw any lump sums beyond the 10 per cent maximum.

If you have an SMSF you need to make sure your trust deed allows for TRISs and, if not, you need to update your trust deed (which will cost around $250 to $500). You will also need to ensure that you have enough cash inside your fund to pay your pension.

Essentially, your fund will be split into two portions: a pension portion (no earnings tax or CGT) and an accumulation portion (continues paying 15 per cent contributions and earnings tax). Because of this, you may need an actuarial certificate (costing upwards of $200) each year to ascertain the member balances, pension balance and accumulation portion. This will help your auditor and ensure that your fund remains compliant. Also note that you cannot contribute money into the pension portion of the fund, only into the accumulation portion, which is why we need to keep this account operational. There are tax benefits in moving most of the assets into the pension phase, owing to the tax concessions afforded to this part of the fund, including no liability for earnings tax and no capital gains tax. The accumulation portion continues to attract 15 per cent contributions tax, 15 per cent earnings tax and capital gains tax of 10 per cent if assets are held for more than 12 months (15 per cent on assets held for less than 12 months).

Case study: transition to retirement income stream

Using our earlier example of Judy, let's say Judy is now 55 and still earning $75 000 per year, with her employer putting in 9 per cent of her salary as superannuation guarantee contributions. Judy now has $350 000 in her super fund, made up of $100 000 non-taxable and $250 000 taxable components (check your annual member statement to get these figures or talk to your super fund).

Our aim is to increase superannuation contributions to the maximum and leave cash flow unaffected so Judy feels no financial pain. We assume that Judy needs all her cash for spending on essentials, as she is now single and needs $57 000 per year to meet her expenses. Her end result will be quite different because of her need for increased cash flow.

Judy could commence a TRIS and draw $32 500 per year from her account until age 65. Judy's cash flow position will remain exactly the same, but she will save around $5000 a year in tax and build her super by contributing 33 per cent more to her super than if she had done nothing. In her case, that means an additional $159 100 in super fund at age 65. Judy has incurred no financial pain as her cash flow had been the same.

If Judy drew less from her TRIS and contributed her full $50 000 to super (including her superannuation guarantee amount, which may fall owing to a reduced taxable income), assuming salary rises over time, she would be significantly better off than the illustrated example. However, we have assumed that her cash flow requirements are the same and I want to illustrate that you can make a big difference by implementing a TRIS strategy without any cash flow pain. Table 12.4 shows the tax components of Judy's super account at present.

Table 12.4: tax components of Judy's super account

Component	Component ($)	Component (%)
Non-taxable component	$100 000	29 %
Taxable component	$250 000	71 %
Total	$350 000	100 %

Note: Assumes a 5 per cent per year return on funds.

Table 12.5 shows the effect of withdrawing the TRIS from Judy's current super account.

Table 12.5: effect of withdrawing TRIS from current super account

Drawdown (%)	Drawdown ($)	Non-taxable component	Taxable component	15 % rebate*
4 % (min)	$14 000	$4 000	$10 000	$1 500
10 % (max)	$35 000	$10 000	$25 000	$3 750
Actual drawdown	$32 500	$9 286	$23 214	$3 482

* This is the amount of Judy's 15 per cent rebate that she receives from TRIS because of her taxable component.

Table 12.6 shows the effect on Judy's income when she takes part of her income as a TRIS. You will see that by taking a TRIS of $32 500, Judy's tax bill has fallen by $5067, and she ends up with an annual income only $433 less than if she lived on her income from her job alone. In the meantime, her super is also growing faster — less tax, more super.

Table 12.6: effect of Judy taking part of her income as a TRIS

	Income	Tax	Net income
Income	$75 000	$17 125	$57 875
TRIS	$69 500	$12 058	$57 442*
Difference		$5 067	($433)

* Including deduction of rebate from Judy's total tax liability.

Table 12.7 shows what is happening in Judy's super account as she draws down her TRIS and adds concessional contributions every year until she reaches age 65. At 65, Judy meets a condition of release and gets full access to her super, even if she is still working.

Table 12.7: effect of TRIS and concessional contributions until age 65

Age	Super balance	Drawdown	Contributions	End balance*
55	$350 000	$32 500	$35 131	$370 262
56	$370 262	$32 500	$35 131	$391 537
57	$391 537	$32 500	$35 131	$413 876
58	$413 876	$32 500	$35 131	$437 332
59	$437 332	$32 500	$35 131	$461 960
60	$461 960	$32 500	$35 131	$487 821
61	$487 821	$32 500	$35 131	$514 974
62	$514 974	$32 500	$35 131	$543 484

(cont'd)

Case study: transition to retirement income stream *(cont'd)*

Table 12.7: effect of TRIS and concessional contributions until age 65 *(cont'd)*

Age	Super balance	Drawdown	Contributions	End balance
63	$543484	$32500	$35131	$573421
64	$573421	$32500	$35131	$604854
65	$604854	$32500	$35131	$637858

* Assumes a 5 per cent per year return on funds.

People who don't need the cash flow or to put in the full $50000 super contribution should understand that all investment earnings in the TRIS account are free of capital gains tax, income tax and earnings tax. So even if you don't need the cash flow from the TRIS, it can be a good idea to withdraw it and contribute it back into your or your partner's super fund as a non-concessional contribution (up to $150000 a year, or $450000 under the three-year averaging rule).

For even higher net worth clients, such as professionals, self-employed people or top level executives, it may not be worth drawing a TRIS, but in most cases, a TRIS will reduce earnings tax and capital gains tax to zero, and boost your super. Taking a TRIS may also be an opportunity to build your partner's super if they have a smaller balance than you. It's a good idea in these circumstances to get expert professional advice and get someone to talk through the opportunities and do some calculations for you so you can accurately determine the benefits of a TRIS.

> **Tip**
>
> A TRIS is all about reducing your tax and boosting your or your partner's super. It's a no-brainer if you are aged 55 to 64, so don't delay and seek advice if you need help.

Strategy 5: account-based pensions— a no-tax investment environment

An account-based pension is an income stream established from your superannuation account once you have reached a full condition of release — such as retirement after reaching the age of 55, or reaching age 65 even if you are still working). The key benefits of an account-based pension are:

¤ you pay no capital gains tax on the sale of assets in your super fund whether you are under or over age 60 in an account-based pension mode

¤ you pay no tax on the investment earnings in your pension account whether you are under or over age 60 in an account-based pension mode

¤ you can take out lump sums of any amount, whenever you want

¤ your reversionary dependent beneficiaries can receive your pension tax-free after your death

¤ there is flexibility as to the type of investments you can make

¤ you pay no tax when you roll over your super money from accumulation mode to pension mode

¤ once you are over the age of 60, all income from your super is free of tax but under age 60 (ages 55 to 59) your super income will be subject to tax, but you also receive a 15 per cent rebate on your taxable portion so many people don't pay tax even under age 60.

In an account-based pension, you have to draw at least a minimum amount of 4 per cent (3 per cent in 2011–12) of your account balance at 1 July or the anniversary of your set-up date every year. You don't have to put all of your money in your super fund into the account-based pension account. You can leave some of your funds in accumulation mode, though you will need an actuarial certificate to segregate your assets if you do this. That means you can go on contributing to your accumulation account while drawing an income stream from your pension account. You can also have multiple account-based pensions.

Case study: account-based pension

Brad is 62 years of age and decides to retire with $1 000 000 in his member balance in his SMSF. Brad and his wife, Anne, need $50 000 a year to meet their expenses, so Brad decides to draw that amount from his account-based pension starting 1 July (you can commence one any time). Brad will draw down

(cont'd)

Case study: account-based pension *(cont'd)*

$4166 per month by establishing a direct debit facility from his investment account in the name of his SMSF to his joint bank account with his wife.

Brad's invested $1 million will be free of earnings tax and capital gains tax, and the $4166 he draws each month will also be free of income tax. In fact, Brad won't even need to file a tax return any more, assuming he has no other taxable income. If Brad needs $30 000 to buy a new car or renovate his bathroom, he can draw the money out of the fund without paying any tax and at any time.

If Brad wants to go back to work, he can, and his account-based pension can remain in place with all its tax benefits. If he does go back to work, Brad may want to salary sacrifice into his wife's super account to build her super balance. As you can see, account-based pensions are very flexible and very tax effective.

Tip

Account-based pensions for over-60s are free of income tax, earnings tax and capital gains tax— there is no better investment environment.

Strategy 6: re-contribution strategy to reduce tax for under-60s and the death tax

The general principle of the re-contribution strategy is to reduce income tax on account-based pensions for people under the age of 60 and to try to lower the death tax. The death tax comes into play when beneficiaries who are not financially dependent on you have to pay 16.5 per cent tax on the taxable portion of your super benefits paid after your death. The aim is to decrease your taxable component and increase your non-taxable component. Your taxable component is created from your 9 per cent employer superannuation guarantee contributions and your salary sacrificed concessional contributions (currently limited to $50 000 for over-50s and $25 000 for under-50s). Your non-taxable portion is created from non-concessional contributions (currently limited to $150 000 a year or $450 000 averaged over three years) that you have made over the years or any pre-1983 contributions you have previously made.

Given that the first $165 000 of the taxable component of your super benefit can be withdrawn tax-free from your superannuation fund once you have met a condition of release, the re-contribution strategy recommends you withdraw that amount in proportion with your non-taxable amount and re-contribute the money back into your SMSF. This will then change the nature of that contribution from a taxable component to a non-taxable component.

The effect of recycling your money in super is that if you want to draw an account-based pension before the age of 60 (when it becomes tax-free in any case), you will reduce the amount of tax to be paid because the non-taxable portion does not attract income tax. The other reason for increasing the non-taxable portion is that the non-taxable component is not subject to death benefits tax in the hands of non-dependants, thus decreasing tax for your beneficiaries when you die.

Case study: re-contribution strategy

Geoff has $450 000 in his superannuation fund. It is made up of 100 per cent taxable component as all his contributions have been from salary sacrifice (concessional contributions). If Geoff dies and passes these assets on to his adult and independent daughter, she will pay 16.5 per cent in tax on the full $450 000. Geoff is retired but under age 65, so he is entitled to contribute up to $450 000 into his super fund as a non-concessional contribution (over three years, or in one year if he takes advantage of the bring-forward rule). While Geoff can't get access to all of those funds in his super without paying some tax on withdrawal, he is entitled to withdraw up to $165 000 tax-free (in 2011–12, but this is indexed and increases each year).

Geoff can withdraw the full $165 000 and re-contribute it to his super. If Geoff was aged between 60 and 64, he could withdraw the lot ($450 000) and re-contribute it into super his as a non-concessional contribution, so his entire account becomes a non-taxable component. This would entirely eliminate the death tax if he died and his super was paid to his non-dependent daughter. Earnings from his investments will become part of the taxable portion of his account, and so would any new concessional contributions, if he went back to work, for instance.

Once Geoff is over age 65, he has to meet the work test (40 hours in any 30 day period in the year in which he wants to make a contribution) to be eligible to contribute to super and he is also restricted to putting in just $150 000 a year as a non-concessional contribution. He cannot use the $450 000 averaging provision because he is over age 65; that means you should use the bring-forward rule just before you turn 65 to make a $450 000 contribution, if you have the cash. If this strategy appeals, you should implement it before you turn 65.

See chapter 9 for more information for those who want to retire before the age of 60 and minimise their tax.

> **Tip**
>
> The re-contribution strategy can reduce your income tax if you are aged from 55 to 59 and drawing a pension, or it can significantly reduce death benefits tax when your super is paid out to non-financial dependants, such as adult children.

Strategy 7: reduce your capital gains tax and maximise your super

This strategy is perfect for people who sell an asset that will realise a significant capital gain outside super. To reduce the effect of capital gains tax, you can contribute cash from the sale of your asset to your super fund and maximise your concessional contributions to reduce your taxable income and therefore your income tax. Under current law, a person over age 50 can contribute $50 000 of concessional contributions to super every year and a person under age 50 can make $25 000 of concessional contributions to super. Keep an eye on my website <www.samhenderson.com.au> for changes to super laws that will affect this strategy. The money you contribute into super will be subject to 15 per cent contributions tax. If the capital gain pushes you into a higher tax bracket, then maximising your concessional contributions can greatly reduce your capital gains tax by reducing your taxable income and therefore the tax payable.

If a couple owned the asset jointly, then both partners can take advantage of the benefits of maximising concessional contributions to super. And if you are over age 50 and under age 65, you can contribute $50 000 each to super to reduce income tax, and up to $450 000 each as a non-concessional contribution to super.

Case study: how to save $23 900 in CGT

Jim and Sue have sold an investment property that they bought in 1999. They paid $500 000 for the property and sold it for $1 000 000 last week, making a capital gain of $500 000. Because they have owned the property for more than 12 months, they receive the CGT discount of 50 per cent, so their taxable gain becomes $250 000. Because the property was in joint names, each of them has a $125 000 taxable gain added to their income for the financial year in which contracts were exchanged (not settled).

My recommendation would be to sell the property after they retire, but before age 65, when they have no other income and they can contribute the money to super as a combination of both concessional and non-concessional contribution limits. Table 12.8 shows how it works. Between them Jim and Sue can save $23 900 if they make $50 000 concessional contributions to their super accounts.

Table 12.8: saving money with concessional contributions

	Jim		Sue	
	Super strategy	Do nothing	Super strategy	Do nothing
Purchase price	$500 000	$500 000	$500 000	$500 000
Sale price	$1 000 000	$1 000 000	$1 000 000	$1 000 000
Capital gain	$500 000	$500 000	$500 000	$500 000
Minus 50% discount	$250 000	$250 000	$250 000	$250 000
Split for joint owners	$125 000	$125 000	$125 000	$125 000
Taxable gain	$125 000	$125 000	$125 000	$125 000
Concessional super contributions	$50 000	$0	$50 000	$0
Contributions tax	$7 500	$0	$7 500	$0
Taxable gain now	$75 000	$125 000	$75 000	$125 000
Tax payable on $75 000	$17 125		$17 125	
Total tax payable	$24 125	$36 075	$24 125	$36 075
Individual tax saving using concessional super contribution	$11 950		$11 950	
Total combined tax saving	**$23 900**			

(cont'd)

Case study: how to save $23 900 in CGT *(cont'd)*

After making concessional contributions to super and putting aside $17 125 each to pay their tax on the remaining capital gain that year, Jim and Sue still have $856 100 left from the sale, assuming agent's fees and other expenses associated with the sale were $20 000. Since they have maximised their concessional contributions ($50 000 each), they can now maximise their non-concessional contributions to super of up to $450 000 each. They could each put $428 050 (half of the $856 100) into super as a non-concessional contribution. The proceeds of the sale of the property are now invested in a tax-free environment if they are in pension phase and over 60, or a concessionally taxed environment if they are under 60.

Tip

Maximise your concessional superannuation contributions to reduce your taxable income and therefore your capital gains tax in the year that you sell an asset. You could save thousands of dollars in tax!

Strategy 8: super splitting to even up a couple's super balances and reduce tax

One of the super provisions the government wants to introduce (it may be law by the time you read this book) is reducing the contribution limits for people who have more than $500 000 in their member accounts. The problem for SMSF members is that the average SMSF has $900 000 in the fund and an average member balance of $450 000, which is pretty close to the $500 000 limit. Compare this with the average super fund balance of around $77 000; the average man currently retires with $150 000 and the average woman retires with $75 000. SMSFs have to manage their members' balances to avoid possible future taxes and restrictions on tax concessions.

My advice is to split superannuation contributions and consider salary sacrificing into your partner's super account if your account balance is close to $500 000 or even $450 000 and your partner's balance is significantly lower. Member balances in SMSFs can be vastly different.

There are several other ways to even out account balances, such as making non-concessional contributions to your partner's account or, at retirement, withdrawing a sum and re-contributing it into your partner's account to increase the non-taxable portion of their member account. If future governments reduce the tax concessions available to holders of large super balances, you know that you have done whatever you can to reduce the damage of unnecessary taxation in the future. While the government has plans to reduce contribution limits, they may have other plans as our workforce ages and tax revenue reduces. Watch this space!

> **Tip**
>
> Super splitting is a useful risk management technique to protect super assets against the possible introduction of new taxes on superannuation.

Strategy 9: borrowing to buy property in your super fund

You can borrow to buy property if you use a limited recourse loan (also known as a property warrant) from a financial institution to meet the provisions in superannuation legislation. A limited recourse loan means that the rest of the super fund assets are not at risk in the event of default on the property loan or instalment warrant. The bank holds only the property inside the instalment warrant as security. Some banks ask for personal guarantees when an SMSF takes out a limited recourse loan, and further security, but most lending products don't.

The beauty of this strategy is that, if you and your partner are both working, you can use tax-effective concessional superannuation contributions to repay the debt. While negative gearing provides a tax deduction, most people I see are still paying an average rate of tax of 30, 37 or 45 per cent on their income, which includes the property rent. This is why many investors use interest-only loans, because they can't afford the cash flow, and they never repay the debt.

There are many advantages to buying a property using a limited recourse loan inside superannuation.

¤   You can pay it off faster with tax-effective super contributions.

¤ The excess rent or cash flow will be taxed at a maximum of 15 per cent if it is cash-flow positive in your SMSF.

¤ Chances are your investment will be cash-flow positive from early on because most banks will lend a maximum of 72 per cent, so you need a 28 per cent deposit to get a limited recourse loan plus the cost of legal fees and other associated purchase costs.

¤ You can sell the property before you retire to get a rate of just 10 per cent capital gains tax if you have owned it for more than 12 months.

¤ You can sell the property in retirement free of capital gains tax.

There are plenty of traps for your SMSF that you must be aware of when it comes to borrowing money and investing in property. You must have the right structures in place, in the form of a limited recourse loan arrangement through a corporate trustee and an underlying trust, which will be the custodian of the asset. As described in chapter 7, you will need these additional corporate trustees and trusts in place in addition to the SMSF and its original corporate trustee. So you will in fact have an SMSF with a corporate trustee and then, sitting underneath that, an additional corporate trustee (custodian of new property) with an additional trust attached (known as bare trust). Once the debt is repaid, the asset moves fully into the SMSF from the name of the custodian, with no capital gains tax liability and no stamp duty payable. You may not use borrowed funds to renovate your property and you cannot substantially change the asset, for instance by subdividing or developing the property into something different. One of the key benefits of this strategy is that when you sell the asset, you will pay just 10 per cent capital gains tax if your super fund is in accumulation mode, or zero capital gains tax if you are pension mode. Given property investment is usually long term and you are probably buying the property to fund your retirement, why would you not buy your next property inside your SMSF? Again, seek advice and make sure you speak with a specialist in this area.

See chapter 7 for a case study of how to buy property in an SMSF.

> **Tip**
>
> See how effective it is to buy property in your SMSF—you can pay it off faster with tax-effective money and you can sell it free of capital gains tax when you're in pension mode (or just 10 per cent CGT if you're in accumulation mode). Much better than negative gearing!

Strategy 10: borrow to buy shares in your SMSF and use your dividends to pay off the debt

You can borrow money to buy shares through your SMSF, in much the same way as you can borrow to buy property. The structure is called an instalment warrant because essentially you can put down a deposit and pay the asset off in instalments over time. The best part about this approach is that you can use the dividends from the shares to repay the debt.

Most providers allow you to borrow to a maximum of 70 per cent of the value of the asset, but I recommend a lower rate of gearing, say 50 per cent, for your first purchase so you can get used to how the product works. Royal Bank of Scotland (RBS), Macquarie, Westpac and Citibank all sell instalment warrants.

Make sure you carefully read the product disclosure statement (PDS) for the product so you fully understand how it works and don't get any surprises. You should also read the warrants pages in the products section of the ASX website <www.asx.com.au> to educate yourself about the use of warrants and the different types available.

Only self-funding instalment warrants are suitable for SMSFs.

Case study: borrowing to buy shares

Let's say you buy a Woolworths share for $28; it pays a 4.5 per cent dividend; and you borrow 50 per cent of its value to buy it. Essentially, you are borrowing $14 and using $14 of your own money. The borrowed $14 will attract interest at, say, 9 per cent a year, and will include a stop-loss order, which means that if the price falls too low, the product supplier will automatically sell the share, or ask you to put more money in. You can lose your money if the share is sold.

Let's say you want to buy $20 000 worth of Woolworths shares, which would be 715 shares at $28, equals $20 020. You would have $10 010 of borrowings at 9 per cent interest, which would be equal to $900.90 per year. Your dividends would be 4.5 per cent of $20 020, which is also $900.90, so the asset would be cash-flow neutral in the first year. Because the shares are franked (meaning the company has paid tax on its profits before it gave you a share of profits in the form of a dividend), your SMSF would also be able to claim back the franking credits when it does its tax return, bringing your pre-tax dividend to 6.42 per cent; however, you cannot use franking credits to reduce your debt. You can repay the debt later if you wish. Ideally, your dividends will rise over time and repay the debt for you, or, as is the case with property, you can use your tax-effective salary sacrifice contributions to repay the debt faster.

For your SMSF, I suggest you choose a conservative share with good dividends. While it is difficult to recommend the right company, companies I would personally consider for myself include Telstra, CBA, ANZ, Woolworths and similar blue-chip stocks that have both growth and income attributes. Additionally, I would suggest you avoid borrowing too much money to buy instalment warrants, as sharemarkets in recent years have been very volatile. Sharemarket down periods might offer good opportunities to buy instalment warrants in good companies at good prices. Timing markets can be difficult, so be careful, stay conservative and remember to allow for share price movements in both the upwards and downwards directions. Risk is never far away, so remember to mitigate risk whenever you can, but don't let it constrain you too much.

See chapter 7 for more detail on how to use instalment warrants.

> **Tip**
>
> Share-based self-funding instalment warrants can literally pay themselves off over time, so if you have five to 10 years before retirement, look into it!

Using and combining these strategies

Use these 10 SMSF strategies to help boost your super and reduce your tax. The first step is to be aware of these strategies and perhaps try one or two to see what the effect will be on your wealth. A client last week immediately saw the benefits of buying property in his SMSF, so he bought two! But I suggest you go slowly and feel your way before you jump headlong into something new.

Once you have mastered one strategy, then you can start adding others and using them in combinations to build significant wealth inside your SMSF. Just be careful and ensure you operate within the realms of the law and that you seek professional advice before you act.

Remember also to read the tax office booklets from <www.ato.gov.au> about how to run an SMSF.

Key points

¤ Salary sacrifice reduces income tax and boosts your super.

¤ Co-contribution is money for nothing from the government if you earn less than $62 000.

¤ If you own a small business, get advice about how to reduce or eliminate capital gains tax (CGT).

¤ Transition to retirement is all about trying to enhance your retirement savings without too much financial pain.

¤ Account-based pensions are a truly tax-free investment environment and the reason you should buy assets inside of your super fund—no income tax, no earnings tax and no CGT!

¤ The re-contribution strategy is designed to save 55 to 59 year olds income tax, and reduce the death benefits tax for non-dependent beneficiaries when you die.

¤ By maximising your concessional contributions in a year in which you sell an asset, you can substantially reduce capital gains tax and boost your super.

- Super splitting can even up member account balances in your SMSF and protect your fund against prospective future changes to taxes on higher balances.

- Property in your SMSF can be paid off faster, be cash-flow positive and sold with no capital gains tax (or, if you are not retired, the CGT can be reduced to 10 per cent if the asset was held for more than 12 months).

- Self-funding instalment warrants allow your SMSF to borrow money to buy shares, and the shares can pay themselves off using the dividends over time.

- Constructing the right strategies should come before choosing the right investments. One of my favourite pieces of advice to clients is 'strategy first, product second'.

- Remember that borrowing money will increase risk, but that risk can be substantially reduced if the debt is reduced. You can do this by maximising your annual tax effective concessional superannuation contributions.

- Use super to build your investments and reduce your income tax.

- These strategies will supercharge your SMSF and help you retire with more money in your pocket!

CHAPTER 13

Financial planning and next steps

Inspiration is a guest who does not like to visit lazy people.
Pytor Ilyich Tchaikovsky, Russian composer

The final chapter in this book is dedicated to making sure you haven't wasted your time in reading my 60 000 words of wisdom. You now need to take action and do something. Whether it's setting up an SMSF to get you started or making sure you have the right documentation in place to run your fund more effectively or just trying some of the SMSF strategies suggested in this text, I'd love it if you actually made some money from my suggestions.

The mere fact that you have bought this book is testament to your desire and motivation to want to make a change, so now is the time to begin that journey. I have no doubt that, if you follow my strategies, you will become wealthier and that wealth may bring with it many more choices to improve your standard of living and that of your family and community. Your SMSF is just one part of a greater financial strategy to help you reach your financial goals.

Figure 13.1 (overleaf) illustrates the important areas of financial planning that you need to consider in concert with your SMSF strategies. One missing area is aged care, but all of the areas shown in the diagram are covered in my first book, *Financial Planning DIY Guide*. You might already have read it as a prelude to this SMSF guide, as the two books are closely correlated and equally important. If not, you will find it covers the areas in the diagram that you need to think about to reach all your financial goals — not just your super and retirement goals.

Figure 13.1: a comprehensive view of financial planning

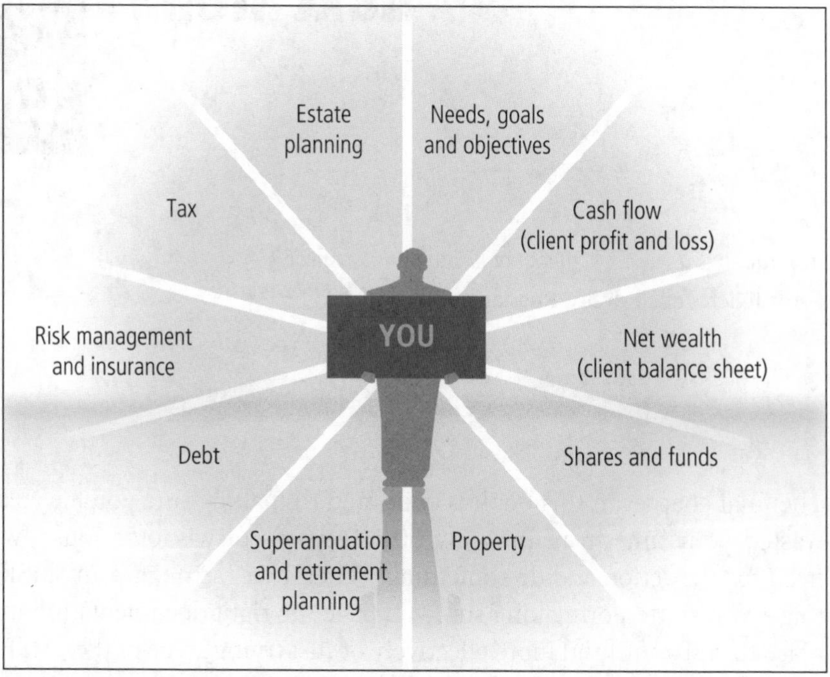

Source: <www.samhenderson.com.au>.

Financial planning

Financial planning will give you a better knowledge of your current financial situation, which will allow you to construct a set of achievable goals and financial objectives. If you don't understand where you are at present, it is difficult to build a plan to allow you to reach your goals. I believe that financial planning begins with a gap analysis of understanding where you are now and how you will achieve your goals and objectives. Without this analysis, you will be paralysed by indecision, and inertia will set in — ensuring failure.

Seven steps to financial success

Figure 13.1 illustrates the process that needs to be followed for you to successfully achieve your goals. You need to understand where you are now and where you want to be in a particular time frame. You then need to set about establishing a number of strategies and tactical responses to help you achieve those goals and objectives. There are seven essential steps to follow:

¤ Build your team.

¤ Work out where are you now (situation analysis).

¤ Work out where you want to be (goals and objectives).

¤ What do you need to do to get there? These are your strategies.

¤ How will the strategies be implemented? These are the tactics you will use to successfully implement your strategies.

¤ Implement the strategies—just do it!

¤ Review and adjust.

Step 1: build your team

If you need help reviewing and adjusting your financial plan then you should seek help from your accountant, financial adviser or stockbroker. No doubt, you will to build a team of professionals to help you with various aspects of your SMSF and financial plan. For example, if you need life insurance, you will need a life insurance broker or a financial adviser. If you need administration completed for your SMSF, you will need an administrator or accountant. Gathering a team is an important part of your success.

Don't try to do everything yourself, particularly when you are starting out. You will need help. Your team will be there to help you and keep you on track. You need to view their fees as a way to create value for yourself and you may use them more at the start while you build your own knowledge and understanding of the various areas involved with running your SMSF or financial plan. Here are some team members you might need:

¤ accountant to set up SMSF, establish corporate trustee, do personal tax returns, and general SMSF administration

- ¤ financial adviser for SMSF set up, writing investment strategy and portfolio management

- ¤ solicitor for conveyancing for properties the SMSF might buy, preparing wills and powers of attorney, testamentary trusts, and setting up guardianship documents

- ¤ insurance broker for life, total and permanent disability, trauma and income protection cover

- ¤ real estate agent for property sales and management

- ¤ stockbroker or online broker for buying and selling shares.

Step 2: where are you now?

There are two parts to this process and it is exactly the same as undertaking due diligence and building a thorough understanding of a business. Having bought several businesses, the first thing I always look at to get an understanding of a business is the profit and loss statement, now officially called a statement of financial performance. As a first step, you need to do a budget and make a register of your assets and liabilities. It's really very simple and easy to construct.

If you visit my website at <www.samhenderson.com.au>, you can download my budget template in either PDF or Microsoft Excel format to use for your own register. Excel format will allow you to use the program's built-in calculators to work out your monthly and annual expenses. This will give you a better understanding of how much you can contribute to super without impinging upon your lifestyle. It's important to find the balance between saving more money and enjoying yourself. There is no point in having money if you can't enjoy it or as I have heard before, 'there is no point in being the richest man in the cemetery'.

The word 'budget', however, can be a swear word for some people! Few people want to hear the word let alone undertake the arduous task of filling in those little cells in the spreadsheet with their annual expenditure. Apart from bringing out the fun police and raining on your parade, a budget will tell you a story about how you spend your money and where your current priorities and obligations lie. It will also show you your financial strengths and weaknesses. Once you are armed with that fundamentally important information from your budget, you will be motivated to do two things that will change your financial life. They are:

¤ increase your income

¤ decrease your expenses.

Step 3: your goals and objectives—where do you want to be?

This sounds really simple, and conceptually it is, but you need to take specific and measurable steps in order to meet your financial goals and objectives. So once you know where you currently stand with your financial budget, write down some goals and objectives remembering to ensure that they have a time frame and are quantifiable. These are called smart goals, and SMART is an acronym for Specific, Measurable, Achievable, Realistic and Timely. Sorry to sound like Anthony Robbins, but if you don't write down your goals, they don't exist. An example may be that you want to retire in 10 years with $1 million in your super fund and a total income of $65 000 a year.

So let's give it a try in table 13.1.

Table 13.1: my goals and objectives

		Value $	By when?
1			
2			
3			
4			
5			

Are your goals SMART?

Tick the box where appropriate:

☐ Specific

☐ Measurable

(cont'd)

Are your goals SMART? *(cont'd)*

☐ Achievable

☐ Realistic

☐ Time-frame bound

Step 4: what do you need to do to get there?

In chapter 12 I described 10 super strategies for your immediate use, and the tactical aspects of how to commence the implementation of those strategies. That being said, strategic direction will be different for everyone, depending upon age, sex, life-stage, income, asset level and a whole bunch of other personal variables that will be specific to your situation.

Now write down your strategies that you would like to put in place (you can get some help from chapter 12). First, you might like to set up an SMSF and commence salary sacrificing. If you are aged over 55 and under 65, you may want to establish a transition to retirement income stream. If you are in your 30s, 40s or even 50s, you may want to borrow money through your SMSF to buy shares or property in an attempt to build your super fund before retirement.

Here are some strategies that you might want to think about:

¤ setting up an SMSF to gain flexibility and more control over your super

¤ salary sacrificing to boost your super

¤ making a non-concessional contribution to super so you qualify for the government co-contribution

¤ making spouse contributions to balance out uneven super account balances and maximise tax-effectiveness

¤ buying a property in your SMSF

¤ buying some blue-chip, high-dividend instalment warrants

¤ setting up a transition to retirement pension (TRIS) once you reach age 55

☐ setting up an account-based pension if you are ready to retire

☐ reducing any capital gains tax liability by maximising your super contributions

☐ using a re-contribution strategy to increase the non-taxable component on your or your spouse's super

☐ using super splitting to balance super accounts between partners and improve tax-effectiveness and boost the lower super balance.

Step 5: how will the strategies be implemented?

Once you have your strategies in a list, you need to construct a list of tactics to implement your strategies. Tactics are practical steps that must be taken to implement your strategies that will allow you to achieve your goals and objectives. For example, here are some tactical steps in setting up an SMSF, and note that they will vary depending on who implements for you and what level of involvement you need to take.

☐ Call your accountant about setting up an SMSF.

☐ Provide your details to your accountant to allow him or her to establish your fund.

☐ Register your SMSF and apply for a tax file number (TFN) and Australian business number (ABN) with the tax office.

☐ Set up a bank account in the name of your SMSF.

☐ Set up a share-trading account with an online broker such as E*TRADE or Comsec, or a stockbroker or financial adviser.

☐ Once your SMSF has been established (it will take at least 28 days), call your current super funds to roll over your current superannuation benefits into your SMSF.

Step 6: implementation—just do it!

It may sound simple but when most people don't know what to do next, they usually just give up. It's no wonder Nike have the slogan, 'Just do it', because that's exactly what you need to do—just do it.

Don't worry about making mistakes: we all make mistakes and that's part of the learning process, and mistakes can generally be fixed.

This is the part where, having decided what you will do (step 4) and how you will do it (step 5), you need to take action. Pick up the phone; open up the internet to start your research; jump in the car and start meeting with people to make things happen. This is often the part when people hit a personal hurdle and inertia sets in and suddenly—nothing happens. You get caught up in your daily routine, meaning to take action, but you just don't have the time, you don't have the money or you don't have the necessary tools to take the next step. Well, don't let procrastination stand in the way of change.

Here's another quote from Anthony Robbins that rings true to me when I think about how many people know what to do but just don't take action, for whatever reason: 'You see, in life, lots of people know what to do, but few people actually do what they know. Knowing is not enough! You must take action.'

Step 7: review and adjust

Once you have begun to implement your strategies, you will need to monitor your progress and review your situation in a time frame that is appropriate to you. I'd suggest you should review your SMSF and your broader financial situation around every six to 12 months so you know where you stand and how you are tracking relative to the goals you set for yourself six to 12 months before. When you see progress—and you will—you will get a sense of self-confidence and empowerment that is inherent in managing your own superannuation and whole financial situation.

Importantly, don't let the performance of property or sharemarkets dampen your resolve. You have little or no control over them and time will take care of their performance in any case. Make sure your strategies are in place and working as you initially set them, and change your asset allocation if you are worried about long-term performance. Remember, when panic is high, opportunity abounds and great wealth has been built through being market savvy and buying good assets at good value when everyone else has taken fright and is selling.

The one-page financial plan

My final solution and gift to you is my one-page financial plan. This is a succinct and concise way of consolidating your financial plan onto one A4 page that can be printed out and posted in a place where you will see it regularly. All of the seven steps I have discussed previously, including constructing a professional team, is contained in the one-page financial plan (see table 13.2, overleaf).

I have included a blank version for you to use and a sample completed version for you to follow on my website <www.samhenderson.com.au>. The completed version is only in PDF format but the blank version is in both Excel and PDF format so you can construct and change your plan however you wish.

Put this plan somewhere you can see it regularly so you remember your goals and objectives. It will be a reminder to stay in control of your finances and constantly review your decisions and progress.

I wish you the best of luck, but remember, don't be afraid to ask for help.

Key points

- ¤ Write down a list of your team members who will help you run your SMSF.

- ¤ Construct a budget to so you can see where you are now financially.

- ¤ Write down your goals and objectives.

- ¤ Develop the strategies you will use to meet your goals.

- ¤ Understand the tactical and practical steps that you need to follow to implement your strategies and get the job done.

- ¤ Follow through—take immediate and decisive action to get your plans under way.

- ¤ Review and implement your financial plan every six to 12 months and make any changes necessary to stay on track to meet your long-term goals.

- ¤ Download the one-page financial plan and follow the steps to create your personalised one-page plan at <www.samhenderson.com.au>.

Table 13.2: the one-page financial plan

	One-page financial plan					Date
1 Team	2 Current situation	3 Goals and Objectives	4 Strategies	5 Tactics	6 Implementation	7 Review of plan
Who is going to help you?	Where are you at now?	What do you want to achieve?	What do you need to do?	What needs to be done to implement the strategy?	Who's involved, contacts, forms done and completed?	By whom, by when, completed?
Financial adviser	Assets	Goal 1-			By whom ___ Contact ___ Forms done Yes No Completed? Yes No	By whom ___ By when ___ Completed? Yes No Review date ___
Accountant	Liabilities	Goal 2-			By whom ___ Contact ___ Forms done Yes No Completed? Yes No	By whom ___ By when ___ Completed? Yes No Review date ___
Solicitor	Net assets	Goal 3-			By whom ___ Contact ___ Forms done Yes No Completed? Yes No	By whom ___ By when ___ Completed? Yes No Review date ___
SMSF administrator	Income before tax	Goal 4-			By whom ___ Contact ___ Forms done Yes No Completed? Yes No	By whom ___ By when ___ Completed? Yes No Review date ___
Stockbroker	Income after tax	Goal 5-			By whom ___ Contact ___ Forms done Yes No Completed? Yes No	By whom ___ By when ___ Completed? Yes No Review date ___
Real estate agent	Superannuation balance	Goal 6-			By whom ___ Contact ___ Forms done Yes No Completed? Yes No	By whom ___ By when ___ Completed? Yes No Review date ___
	Structures	Goal 7-			By whom ___ Contact ___ Forms done Yes No Completed? Yes No	By whom ___ By when ___ Completed? Yes No Review date ___
	Insurances Estate planning	Goal 8-			By whom ___ Contact ___ Forms done Yes No Completed? Yes No	By whom ___ By when ___ Completed? Yes No Review date ___

Glossary

ABN   Australian business number.

account-based pension   A tax-effective retirement income stream commenced with superannuation money.

actuary   A professional mathematician who calculates risk, uncertainty and a host of other specific numbers including tax benefits for SMSFs. You will need one if you have a TRIS or one member has an account-based pension when others are in accumulation mode and assets are not segregated.

actuarial certificate   A certificate of authenticity provided by an actuary to allow you to claim a tax exemption on your SMSF's income stream.

arm's length   An investment transaction that must be undertaken on a commercial basis to avoid mispricing or underpricing of the asset to avoid or limit capital gains tax, stamp duty or other transactional costs.

audit   A process of verification, confirmation and substantiation that certain processes, rules and transactions have actually taken place and reported assets actually exist.

Australian Prudential Regulation Authority (APRA)   The regulator for trustees of public offers, and retail and industry super funds.

Australian Securities Exchange (ASX)   The Australian sharemarket.

ASFA   Association of Superannuation Funds of Australia.

Australian Securities and Investments Commission (ASIC)   The federal regulator of financial services licensing in Australia, and corporations law.

Australian Taxation Office (ATO)   The regulator of SMSFs.

AWOTE   Average weekly ordinary time earnings.

balanced fund   A managed fund or super fund that has between 40 and 70 per cent of assets invested in shares.

binding nomination of beneficiaries   A request via specific form that needs to accompany a trust deed that specifies death benefits be paid out to a nominated dependent beneficiary under SIS Act rules. It is binding on trustees, and trustees have no discretion as to the distribution of assets inside the super fund.

business real property   A property that is an active asset of a small business, i.e. used in the operation of a small business.

capital gains tax (CGT)   A taxable gain from the sale of an asset that is added to normal annual income in the financial year in which one enters the contract of sale (not at settlement in the case of property sales).

Centrelink   A federal government organisation that manages and processes social welfare payments.

CGT discount   If you own an asset for longer than 12 months, it is eligible for a 50 per cent reduction in capital gain. This is designed to make people hold assets for longer.

co-contribution   A government initiative to encourage superannuants to put extra money into their super funds by matching non-concessional contributions for low-income earners.

concessional contributions   Superannuation contributions that have 15 per cent contributions tax payable by the fund. For example, employers' 9 per cent superannuation guarantee amounts or salary sacrifice.

condition of release   A proviso that must be achieved to gain access to superannuation such as reaching age 55 or 65, retirement, death, disablement, financial hardship, permanently leaving Australia, balance under $200, transition to retirement (TRIS).

consumer price index (CPI)   The rise or fall in prices of a general basket of goods and services representative of a whole market or economy.

contribution limits   The maximum amount you can put into super (concessional or non-concessional) without being charged penalty tax.

corporate bonds   Bonds issued by companies that pay a coupon rate (interest rate to investors) that reflects the company's risk profile.

corporate super fund   A super fund operated by a corporation on behalf of its employees.

corporate trustee   A company that acts as a trustee for your super fund.

death tax   The 16.5 per cent tax payable on the taxable portion of superannuation death benefits distributed to non-dependants under tax legislation (ITAA 97).

defined benefit fund   A superannuation fund that has a pre-determined lump sum at retirement or rollover that is a function of one's final average salary. It can also be defined as monthly income for life that is indexed to the CPI and reversionary (66 per cent goes to spouse in event of death).

derivative   An investment that is a secondary product of a primary asset such as a share property that may include options, warrants, CFD or other types of contractual obligations between a product manufacturer and the investor.

dividend   All or part of a company's profit distributed to shareholders on a regular basis, usually every six months.

eligible start date   The first date funds were contributed to a super fund (first superannuation contributions).

financial adviser/financial planner   An authorised representative who operates under an Australian financial services licence issued by the Australian Securities and Investments Commission (ASIC).

fixed interest   Bond and cash-like investments that are invested for a fixed period of time and generally paying a coupon or interest rate to the investor.

franking credit   A tax benefit received from owning shares in a company that has paid company tax on all or part of its income. For example, '100 per cent franked' means all of the company's tax rate (currently 30 per cent) has been paid on the income you receive in the form of a dividend.

gearing   Borrowing money to invest.

GFC   Global financial crisis.

government bonds   Financial products issued by governments to raise capital. These bonds pay investors a coupon rate (interest rate) reflective of the risk of that government.

industry super funds   Not-for-profit super funds originally designed for members of particular industries but which are now open to all members of the public.

in-house asset   An investment in a lease or loaned money to a related party or trust of a fund.

in-specie transfer   An off-market transfer of shares from one entity to another. The government is proposing to outlaw the in-specie transfer of shares from your own name or other entity to your super fund to reduce the risk of avoiding or reducing capital gains tax.

instalment warrant   An investment product designed to be repaid over a period of time.

investment strategy   A written document that details how the assets of the SMSF will be invested according to the trust deed and risk attitude of members to meet the investment objectives of member trustees.

ITAA   *Income Tax Assessment Act 1997.*

limited recourse loan   A loan that can be secured only with the asset for which the borrowing is intended. The particular asset is the only collateral (security) used by the bank.

management expense ratio (MER)   Also known as an investment cost ratio, this is the underlying cost of a managed fund that is usually included in the unit pricing of the product.

marginal tax rates   The scale of taxation rates applicable to taxable income in Australia as set by the Australian Taxation Office (ATO). These rates change over time.

member statement   An annual summary of an SMSF member's super contributions, superannuation portions, eligible start date and other important personal superannuation details.

non-concessional contribution   A non-taxable superannuation contribution, i.e. it does not attract 15 per cent contributions tax. For example, spare cash from a savings account, an inheritance or from the (after-tax) sale of an asset.

non-preserved, unrestricted   Money in a superannuation fund that can be accessed at any time, even without a condition of release.

non-taxable portion   Made up of the contributions to a super fund that were not taken along the way, such as non-concessional contribution, small business rollover or pre 1983 components. Earnings on non-taxable portions are taxable.

power of attorney   A formal document authorising a person to legally act on another's behalf.

preserved superannuation   Money that is not accessible until a person reaches a condition of release.

probate   The process of identifying that a valid will exists and that the executor has the authority to act on behalf of the estate.

property   Direct investment, residential or commercial dwellings. Property securities (property companies listed on the ASX) are classified as property.

re-contribution strategy   The process of withdrawing taxable money from superannuation and re-contributing it as a non-concessional tax-free contribution. Often used to lower income tax and reduce the death tax.

related party transaction   A purchase, sale or transfer of an asset from an entity that is related to an SMSF.

restricted unpreserved   Superannuation money that may be accessed from a superannuation account under certain circumstances, such as leaving your job. Applies to super contributions prior to 1999.

retirement   Ceasing work once over the age of 55 and working fewer than 10 hours per week.

reversionary beneficiary   A spouse or dependant who will receive a deceased person's superannuation pension in the event of death with all the tax benefits afforded to the deceased.

risk management   The process of attempting to reduce a financial loss.

risk profile   A person's attitude and reaction towards the potential and actual rise and fall of asset prices. For example, a conservative risk profile means one should hold more cash than shares.

salary sacrifice   A concessional contribution (attracting 15 per cent superannuation contributions tax) to a super fund from gross salary.

segregated assets   Some people like to separate the assets of members, especially in the case of pensions, so that member balances and pensions are easier to calculate.

shares   Small units in companies traded on the ASX. All companies, small and large, are made up of shares owned by shareholders.

single member trustee   An SMSF can have a single member but it must have a secondary trustee such as a relative or close friend.

SIS Act   *Superannuation Industry (Supervision) Act 1993.*

Small APRA Fund (SAF)   A small superannuation fund, like an SMSF, that has an external trustee.

sole purpose test   The key purpose of superannuation is to fund retirement and provide retirement death benefits for beneficiaries.

superannuation   A tax-effective investment structure designed to fund retirement.

Super Choice   A federal government initiative allowing employees to contribute to the super fund of their choice rather than having employers choose for them. (Choice is available to members who do not have a contract with their employers as to the super fund they can use.)

taxable portion   The money in your super fund that is made up of contributions that were taxed on the way in (such as salary sacrifice and 9 per cent employer superannuation guarantee amounts). Also includes all earnings of the super fund.

tax return   An annual assessment of taxation that is sent to the ATO by a particular date each year to assess one's taxable position and report on the fund transactions throughout the year as well as member positions.

10 per cent rule   Where 10 per cent or more of your income comes from self-employment. This is also relevant for under-65s who are not working and classified as self-employed for the purposes of making concessional superannuation contributions to reduce capital gains tax.

testamentary trust   A trust that is established on someone's death to manage assets and distribute income that can be tax effective to minors and protect a family's assets.

TFN   Tax file number.

transition to retirement income stream (TRIS)   A retirement income stream that can be started from a superannuation fund between the ages of 55 and 64 where one can draw between 4 per cent (3 per cent in 2012) and 10 per cent of the fund's value each year.

trust deed   A set of governing rules that a super fund must abide by. The federal legislation governing superannuation (SIS Act 1993) takes precedence over the rules of the trust deed.

trustee   A person responsible for making decisions about the operations of a trust. Superannuation is a trust and therefore a super fund needs trustees for the effective and legal operation and investment of the fund.

volatility   An upwards or downwards movement in the value of an asset.

Warren Buffett (the Oracle of Omaha)   An investment guru who has received a 28 per cent year-on-year return since 1954 and one of the world's most successful and wealthiest investors. He is the CEO of Berkshire Hathaway based in Omaha in the United States — an investment company whose A-class shares are now worth over $100 000 each.

work test   If you are over 65 you need to work 40 hours in any 30-day consecutive period to be eligible to contribute either concessional or non-concessional contributions to an eligible superannuation fund.

wrap account   An investment platform used by financial advisers to invest their client's money into shares or managed funds.

yield   The investment return from an asset usually expressed as a percentage. For example, a property investment has a 5 per cent gross yield, or a 5 per cent income before costs.

Index

Also in the DIY Guide series

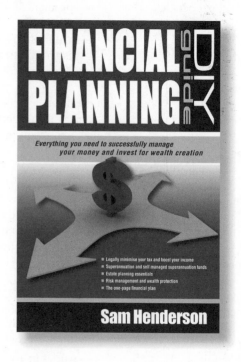

Available from all good bookstores